I0478927

FLAGS
OF THE
WORLD
THE COLORING BOOK
CHALLENGE YOUR KNOWLEDGE OF THE COUNTRY FLAGS!

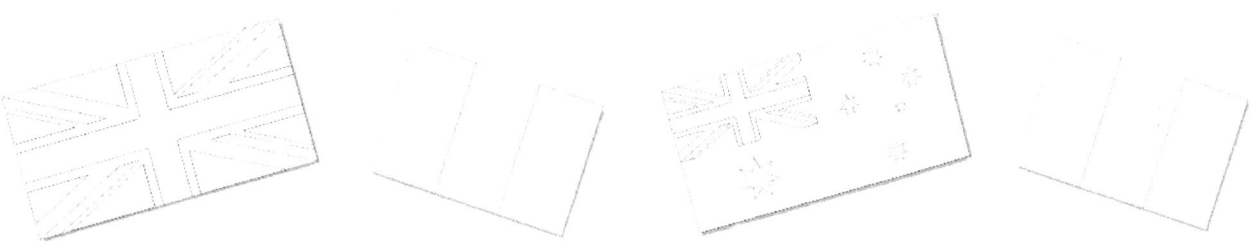

THIS COLORING BOOK BELONGS TO:

_____

_____

B.C. Lester Books
Geography publications for the people since 2019.

Visit us at www.bclesterbooks.com for more!

All flags were correct at the time of publication. This book does not reflect any views of the author or publishing house. No part of this book may be copied, reproduced or sold without the express permission from the copyright owner.

Copyright B.C. Lester Books 2021. All rights reserved.

A MESSAGE FROM THE PUBLISHER

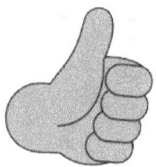

Hey! Thank you for making the purchase, we really hope you enjoy this book. If you have the chance, then all feedback is greatly appreciated. We have put a lot of effort into making this book, so if you are not completely satisfied, please email us at ben@bclesterbooks.com and we will do our best to address the issues. If you have any suggestions, enquries or want to send us a selfie with this book, then email at the same address - ben@bclesterbooks.com

Is this book misprinted? Drop us an email with a photo of the misprint and we will send out another copy!

WHO ARE WE AT B.C. LESTER BOOKS?

B.C. Lester Books is a small publishing firm of three people based in Buckinghamshire, UK. We aim to provide quality works in all things geography, for kids and adults, with varying interests. We have already released a selection of activity, trivia and fact books and are working hard to bring you wider selection. Have a suggestion for us? Then email ben@bclesterbooks.com. We are all ears!

TO COMPLIMENT YOUR FLAG COLORING EXPERIENCE, WE RECOMMEND:

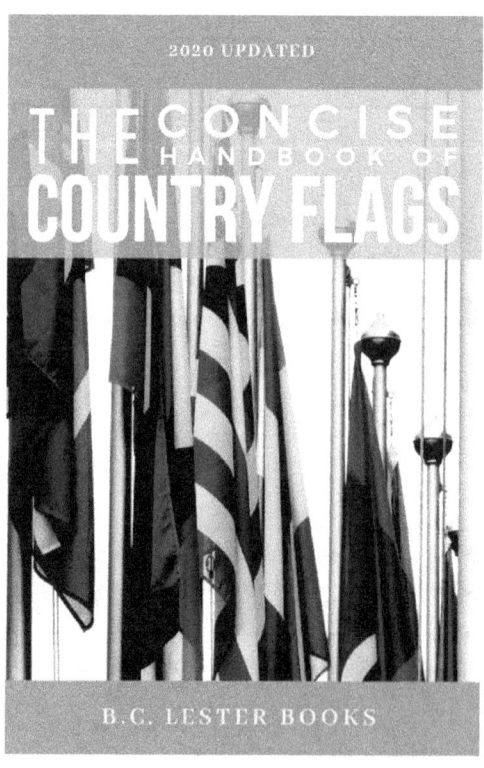

A-Z country flags for a color guide when using this book.

ISBN-10: 1913668231

BEFORE YOU START...

Test your coloring equipment here for bleedthrough. Note that this coloring book is NOT recommended for paint or highlighters...

Some of the flags are quite simple, such as Poland, which is half red and half white... but others a little more complex, such as Kazakhstan, which has this banner incorporated into the flag...

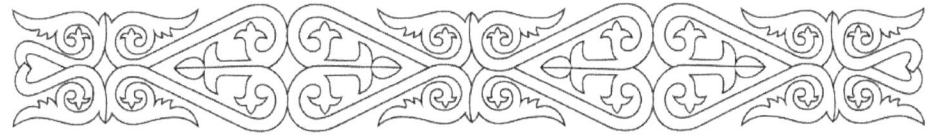

For this reason, we recommend coloring pencils or coloring pens, unless you feel confident with another medium!

NUMBERING SYSTEM & RECOMMEND COLORS TO USE

The flag name corresponds to a number on every double spread. The numbers in a grey square to the right of the name refer to the colors used in the flag (excluding coat of arms where stated). Think of this as more of a hint than a color guide.

1 **FLAG OF THE UNITED STATES**   2   14   16

Also, be sure to check the back cover for the recommended colors to have before starting this book. We have 'rounded up' the shades of all colors that appear in country flags into 16 colors to use within this book (20 if you want to be more detailed with the coat of arms).

ALL GOOD?

Prepare your favorite brew, relax, and enjoy the experience!

B.C. Lester Books

FLAGS OF NORTH AMERICA

A-Z

---

1 FLAG OF ANTIGUA & BARBUDA

2   6   12   15   16

2 FLAG OF BAHAMAS

6   11   15

3 FLAG OF BARBADOS

6   14   15

4 FLAG OF BELIZE

3   9   14   16   *EXCLUDING COAT OF ARMS

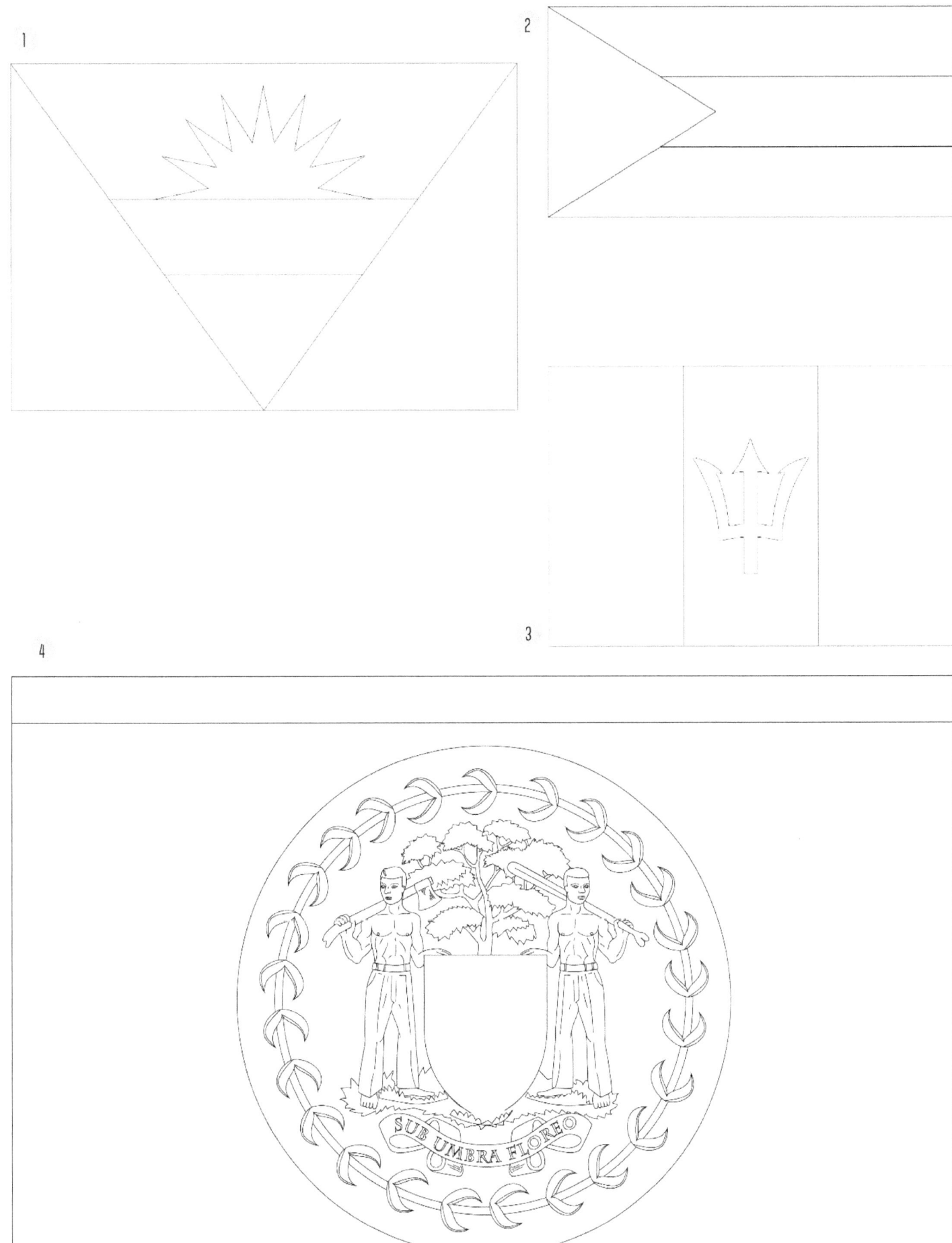

1

2

3

4

1 FLAG OF CANADA

3   16

2 FLAG OF COSTA RICA

2   14   16   *EXCLUDING COAT OF ARMS

3 FLAG OF CUBA

2   14   16

4 FLAG OF DOMINICA

2   7   10   15   16   *EXCLUDING COAT OF ARMS

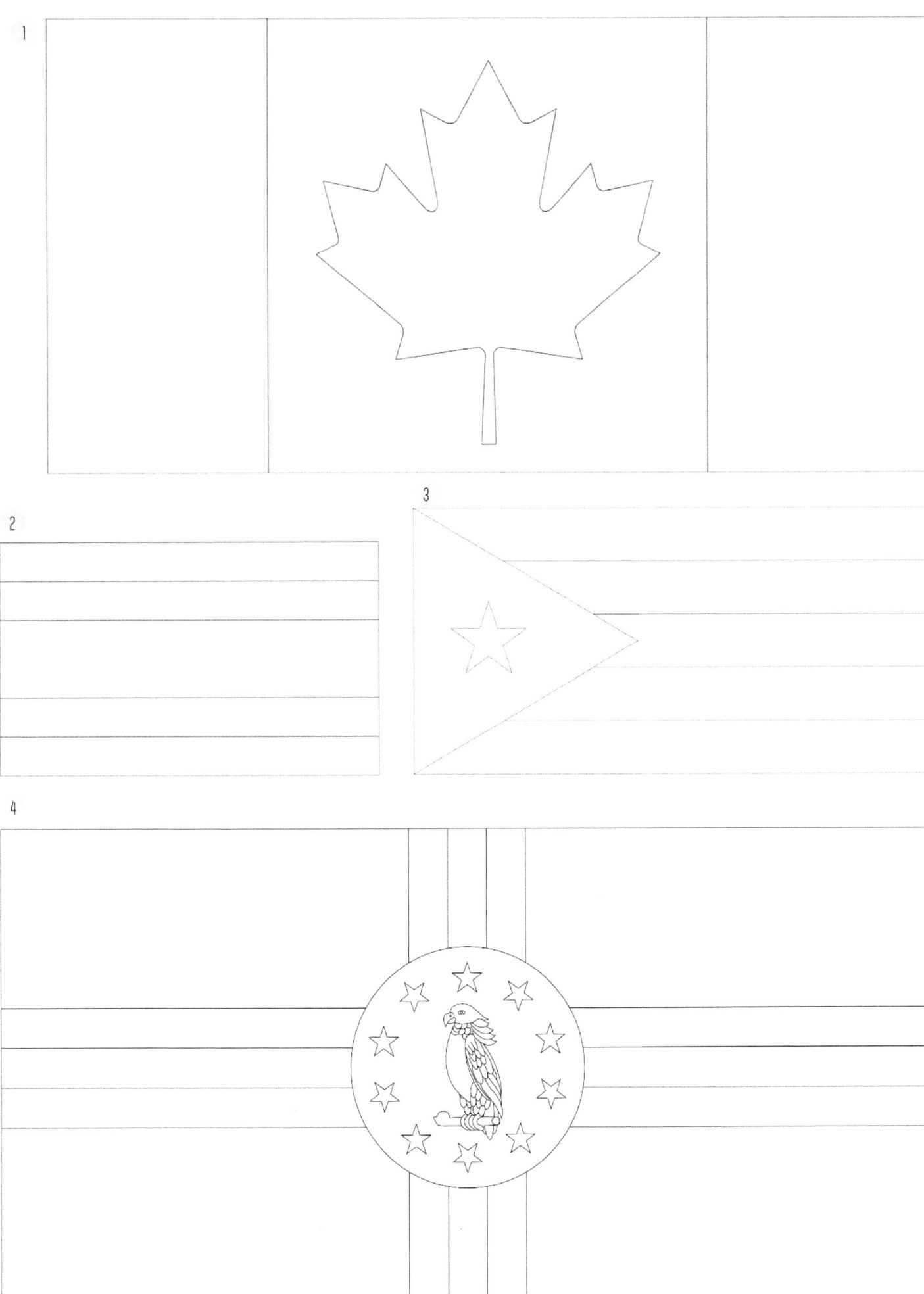

① FLAG OF DOMINICAN REPUBLIC

2   14   16   *EXCLUDING COAT OF ARMS

② FLAG OF EL SALVADOR

13   16   *EXCLUDING COAT OF ARMS

③ FLAG OF GRENADA

2   6   10

1

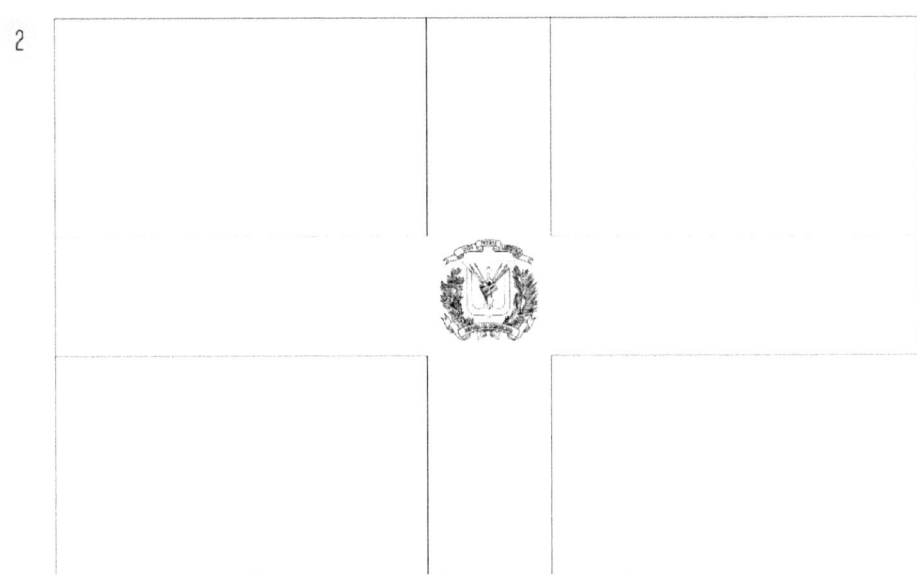

2

3

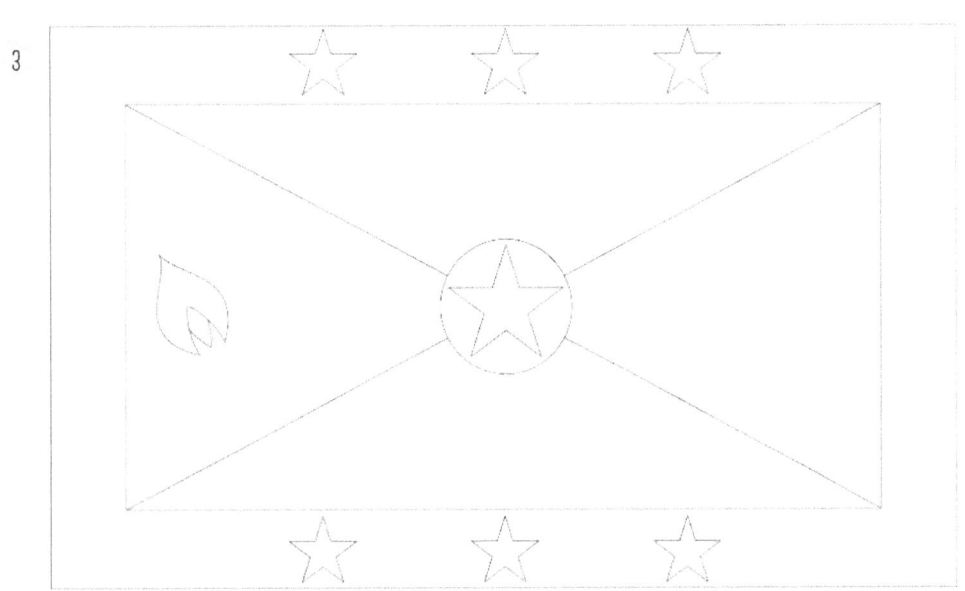

FLAG OF GUATEMALA

11   16   *EXCLUDING COAT OF ARMS

FLAG OF HAITI

2   14   16   *EXCLUDING COAT OF ARMS

1

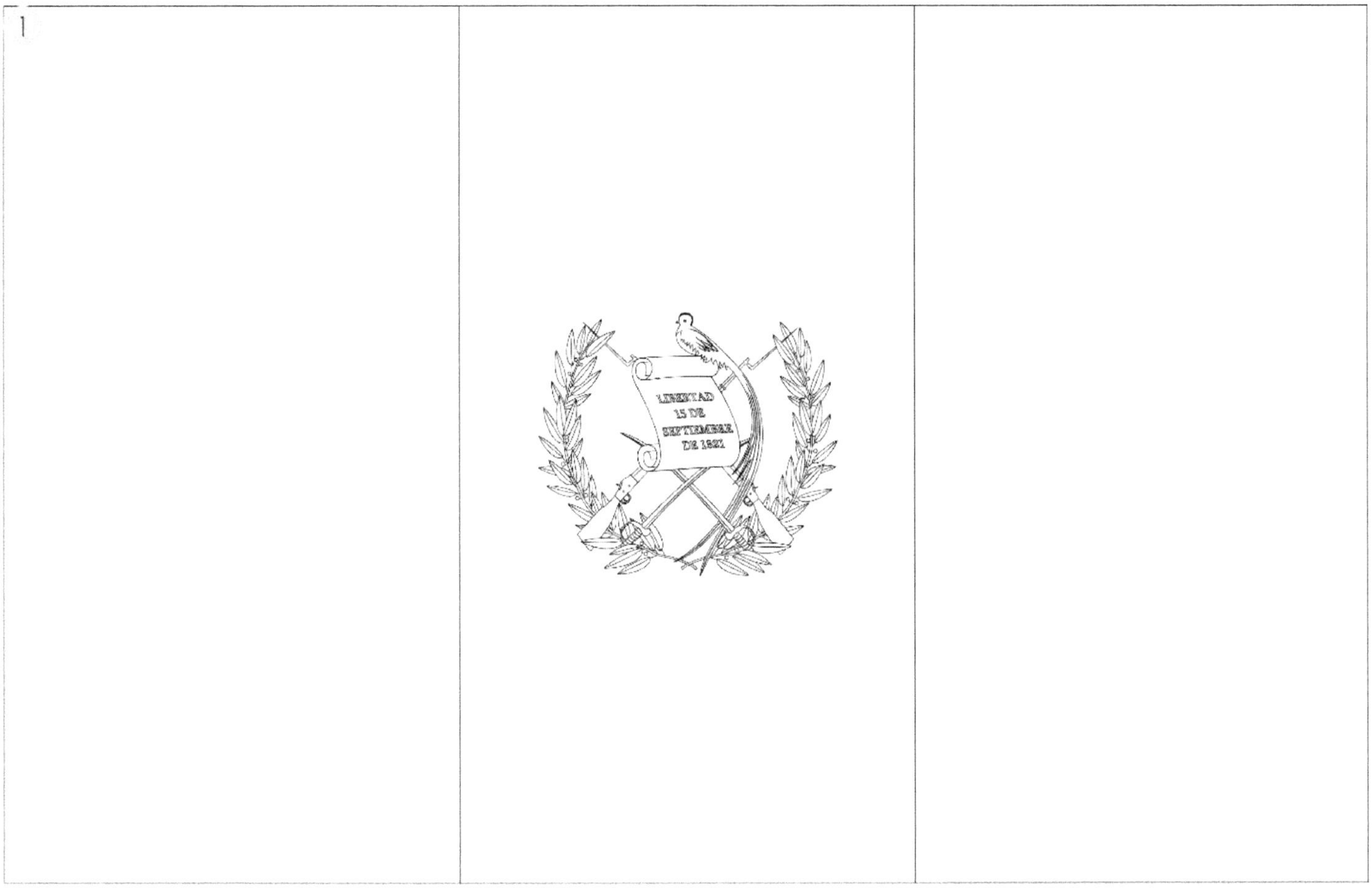

LIBERTAD
15 DE
SEPTIEMBRE
DE 1821

2

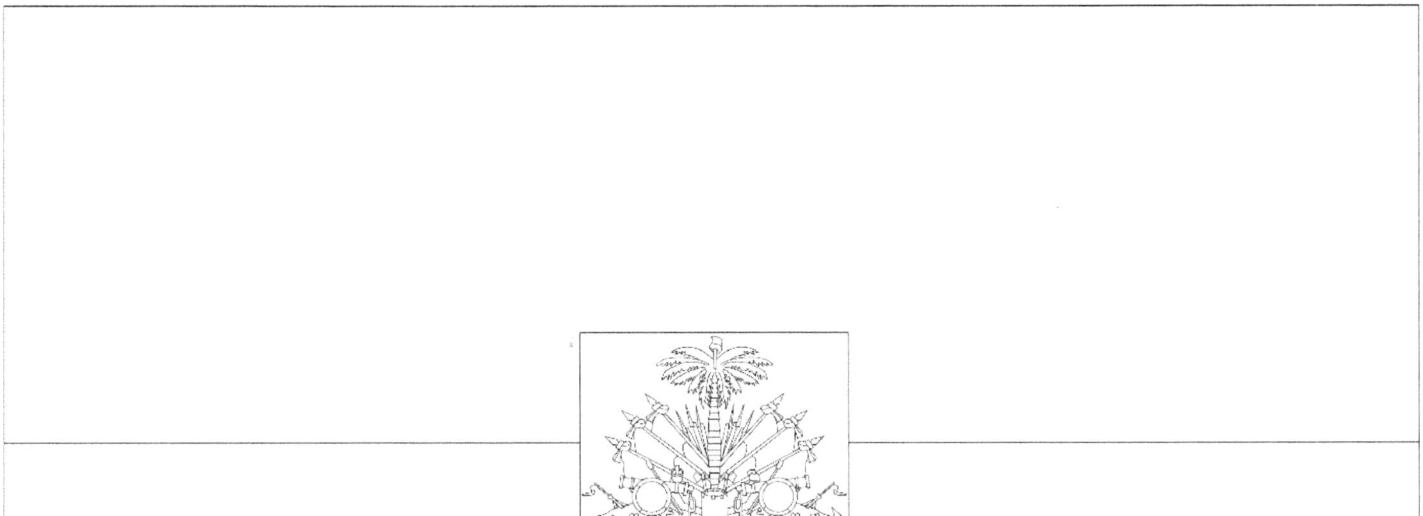

1. FLAG OF HONDURAS

14   16

2. FLAG OF JAMAICA

6   9   15

3. FLAG OF MEXICO

2   10   16   *EXCLUDING COAT OF ARMS

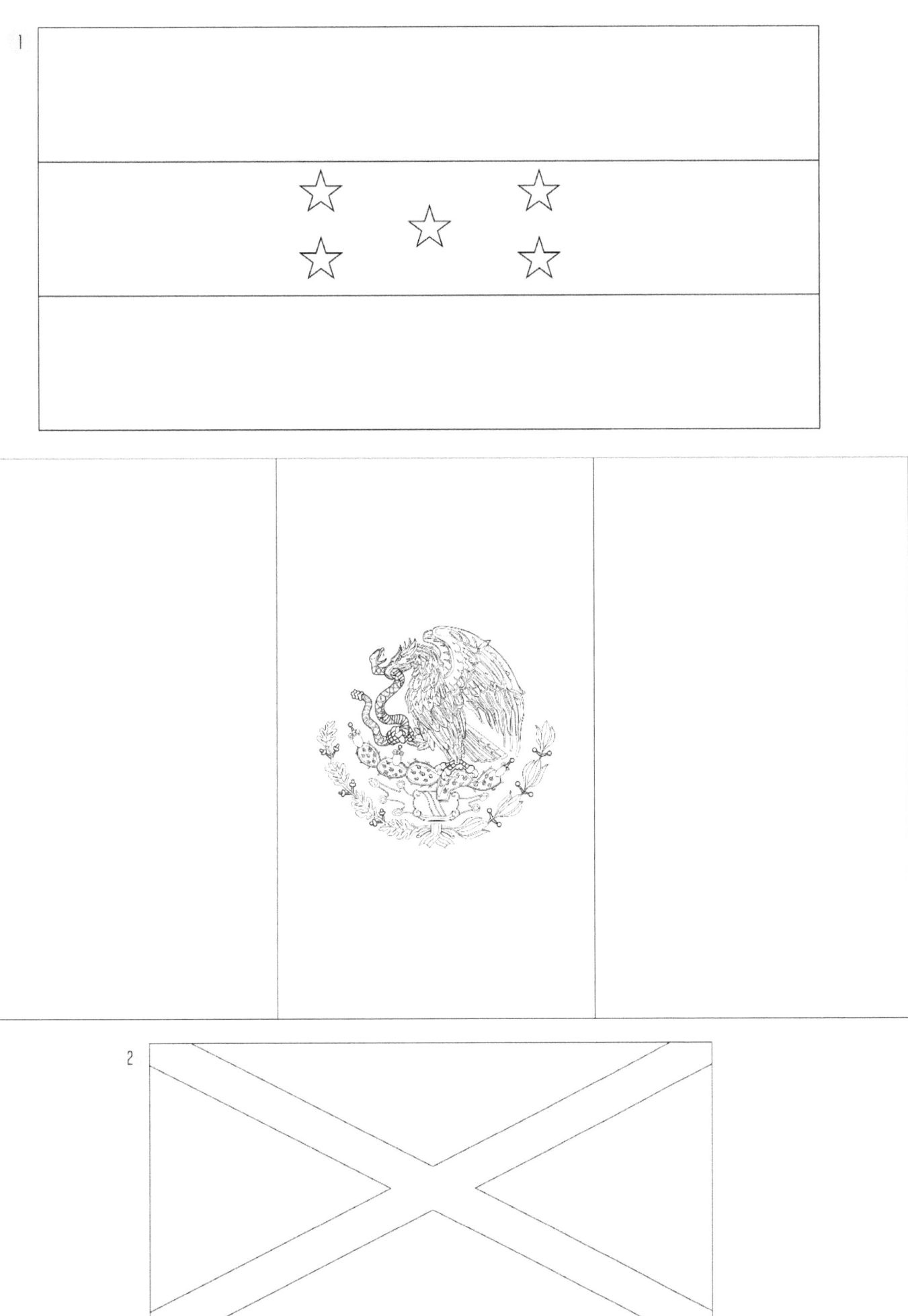

1 FLAG OF NICARAGUA

13   16   *EXCLUDING COAT OF ARMS

2 FLAG OF PANAMA

3   14   16

3 FLAG OF SAINT KITT'S AND NEVIS

2   6   9   15   16

4 FLAG OF SAINT LUCIA

6   11   15   16

2

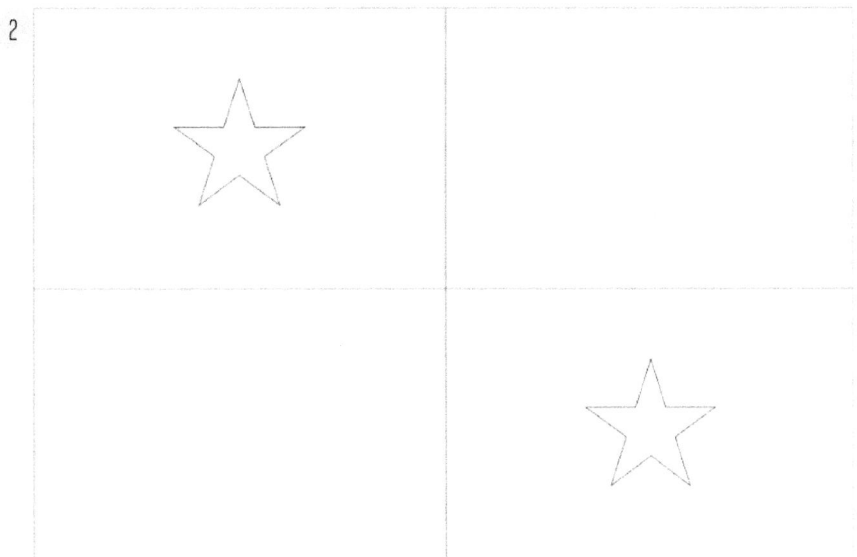

1

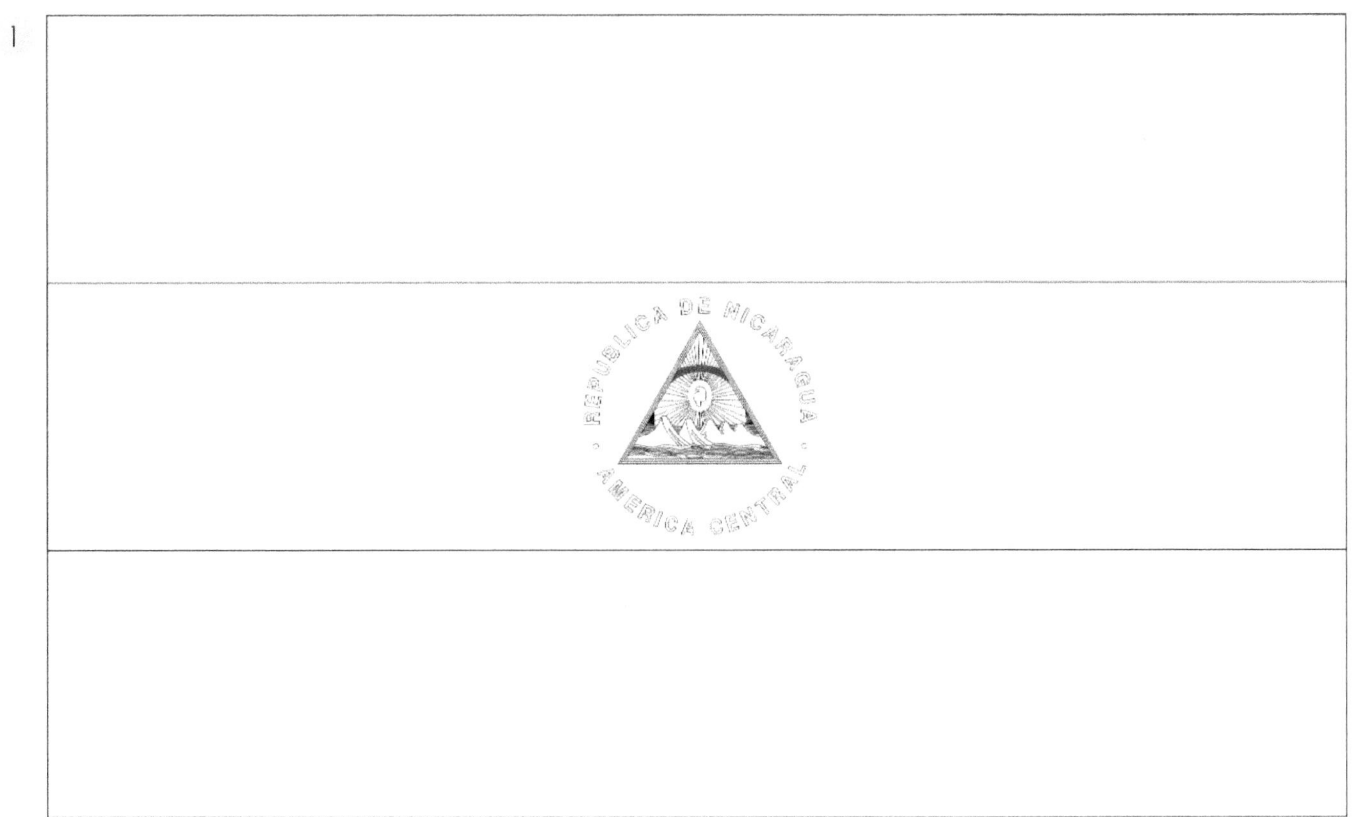

3

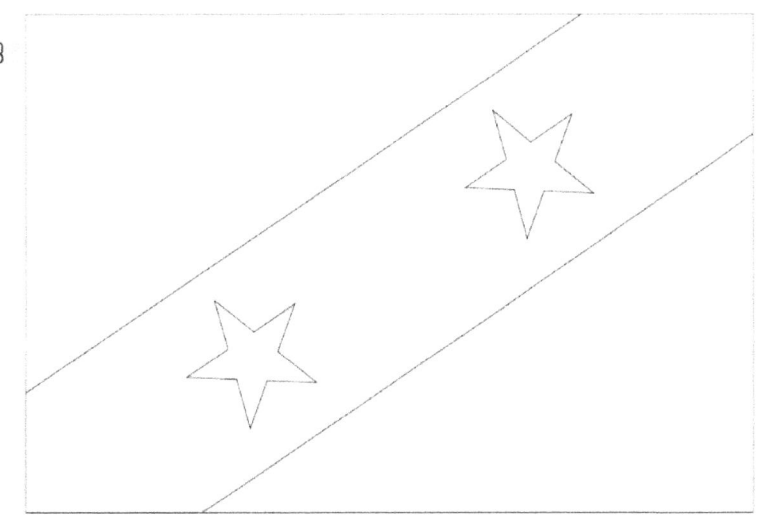

1 FLAG OF SAINT VINCENT AND GRENADINES

6   10   14

2 FLAG OF TRINIDAD AND TOBAGO

2   15   16

3 FLAG OF THE UNITED STATES OF AMERICA

2   14   16

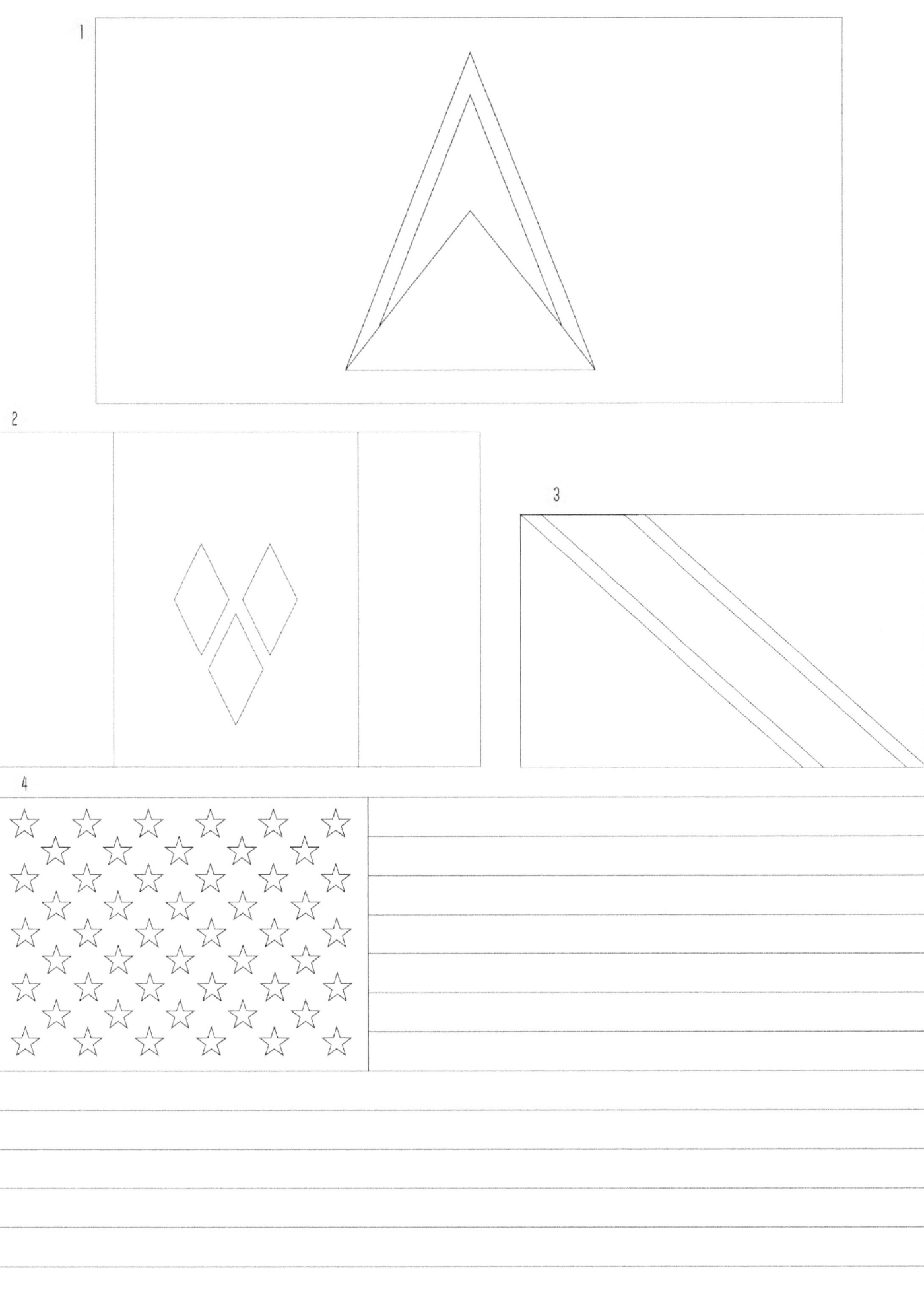

FLAGS OF SOUTH AMERICA
A-Z

1 FLAG OF ARGENTINA
6   11   16

2 FLAG OF BOLIVIA
3   7   10   *EXCLUDING COAT OF ARMS

3 FLAG OF BRAZIL
6   9   14   16

4 FLAG OF CHILE
2   14   16

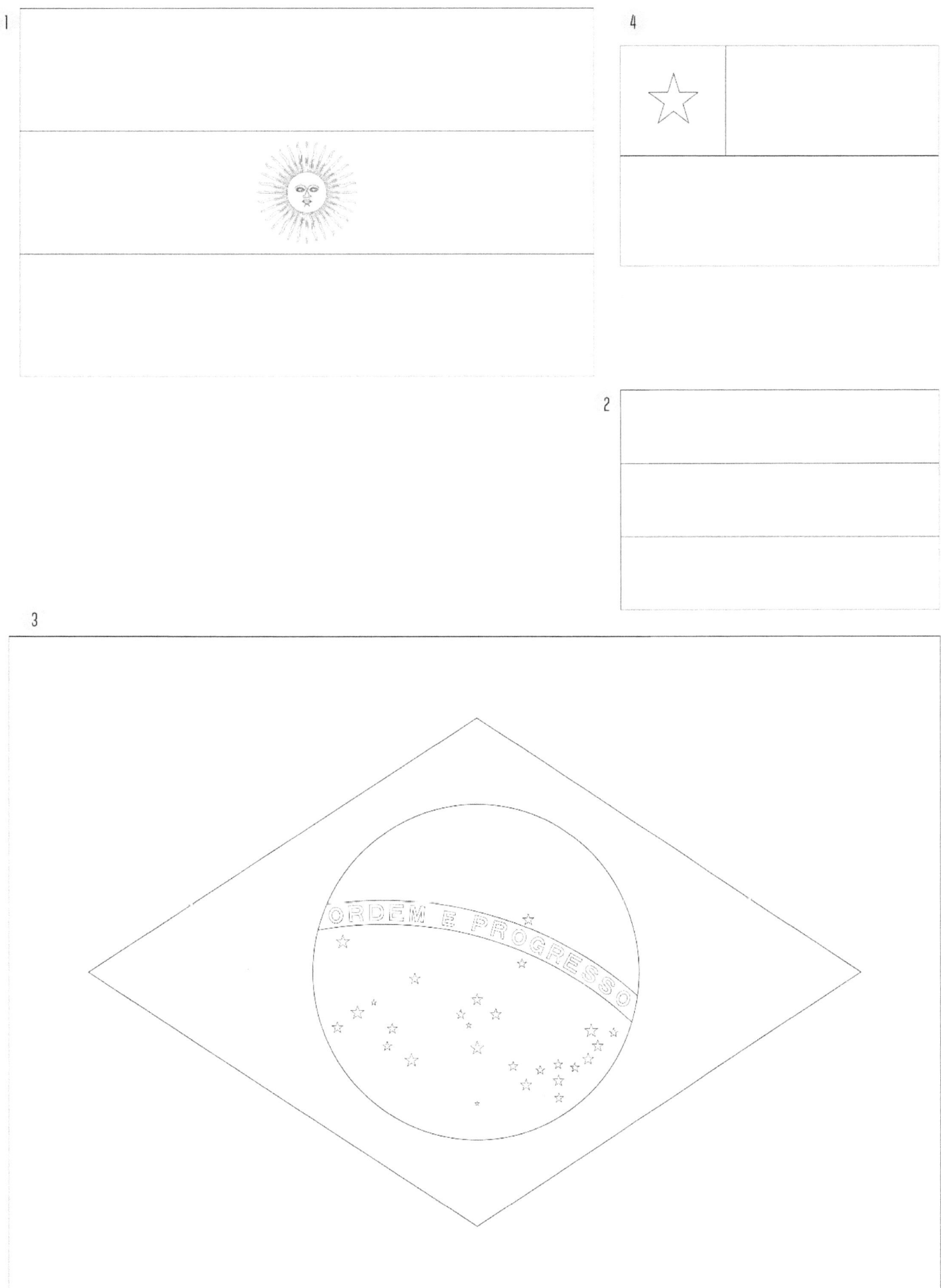

1 FLAG OF COLOMBIA
2   6   14

2 FLAG OF ECUADOR
3   6   13   *EXCLUDING COAT OF ARMS

3 FLAG OF GUYANA
2   6   9   15   16

4 FLAG OF PARAGUAY
2   14   15   16   *EXCLUDING COAT OF ARMS

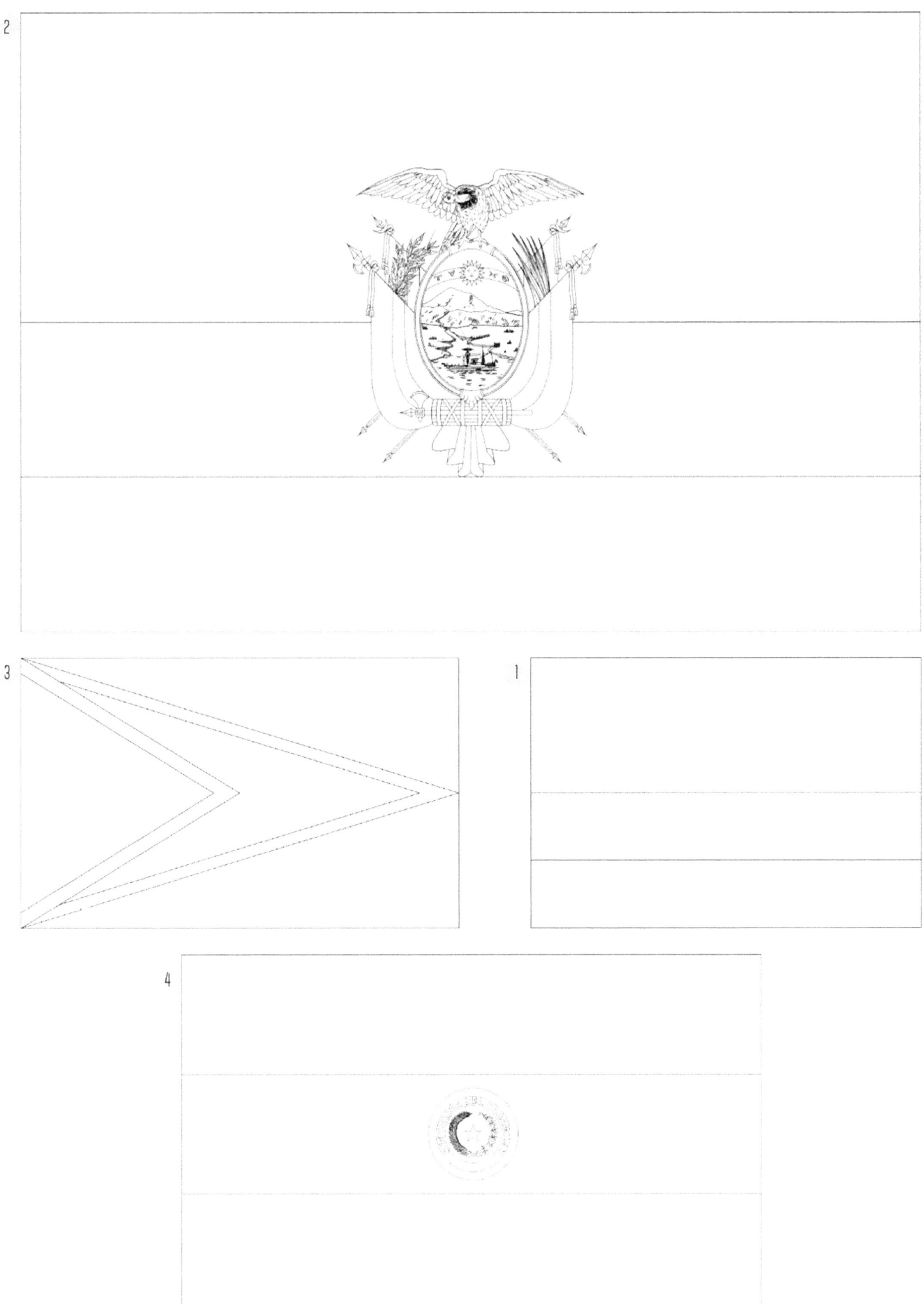

1 FLAG OF PERU

3   16

2 FLAG OF SURINAME

2   6   10   16

3 FLAG OF URUGUAY

5   6   14   16

4 FLAG OF VENEZUELA

2   6   14   16

FLAGS OF AFRICA
A-Z

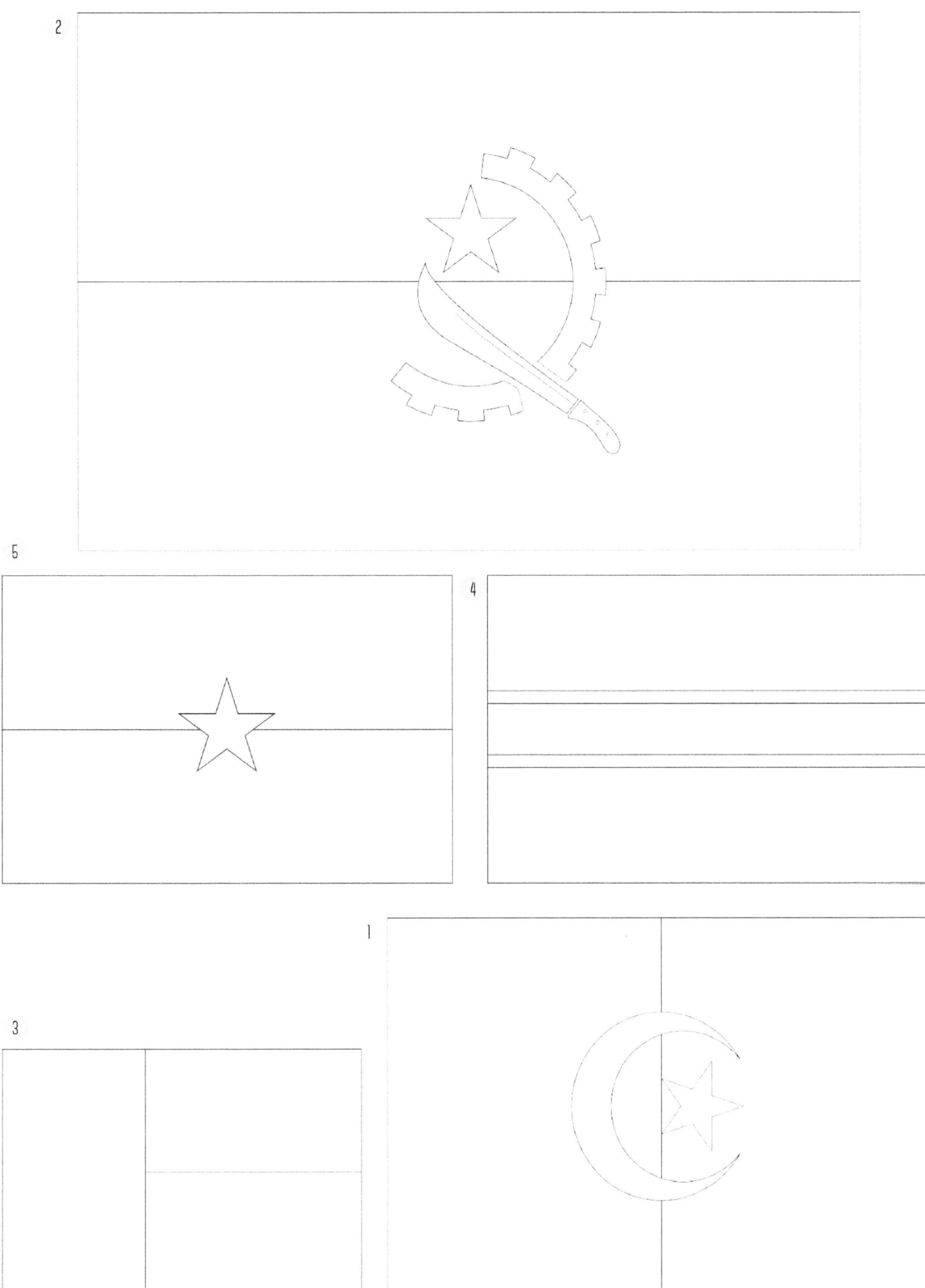

1 FLAG OF BURUNDI

2   8   16

2 FLAG OF CAMEROON

2   6   10

3 FLAG OF CAPE VERDE

2   6   14   16

4 FLAG OF CENTRAL AFRICAN REPUBLIC

2   9   10   15   16

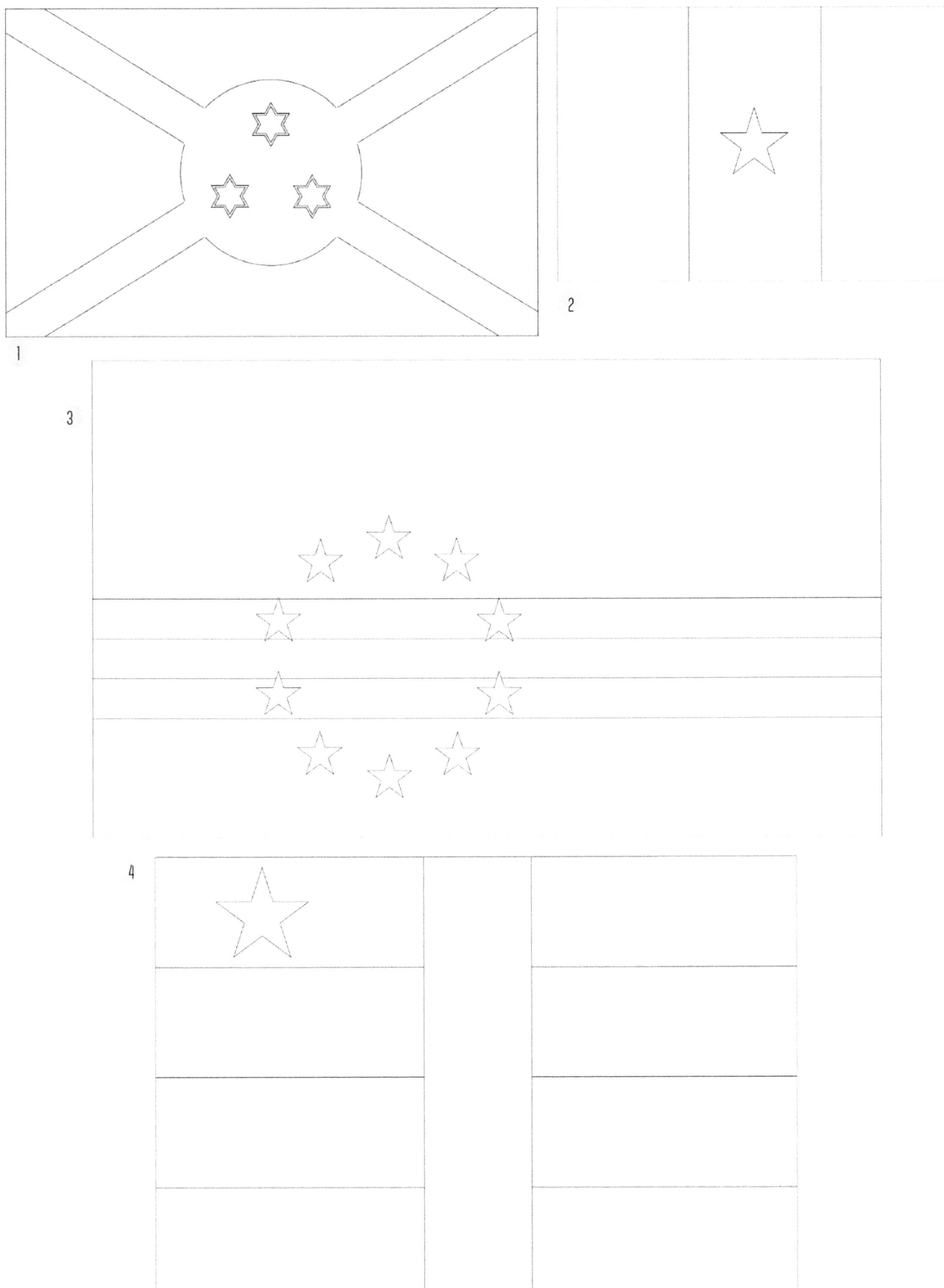

1 FLAG OF CHAD

2   6   14

2 FLAG OF COMOROS

2   6   9   13   16

3 FLAG OF DEMOCRATIC REPUBLIC OF THE CONGO

2   6   12

4 FLAG OF REPUBLIC OF THE CONGO

3   6   9

5 FLAG OF DJIBOUTI

2   8   11   16

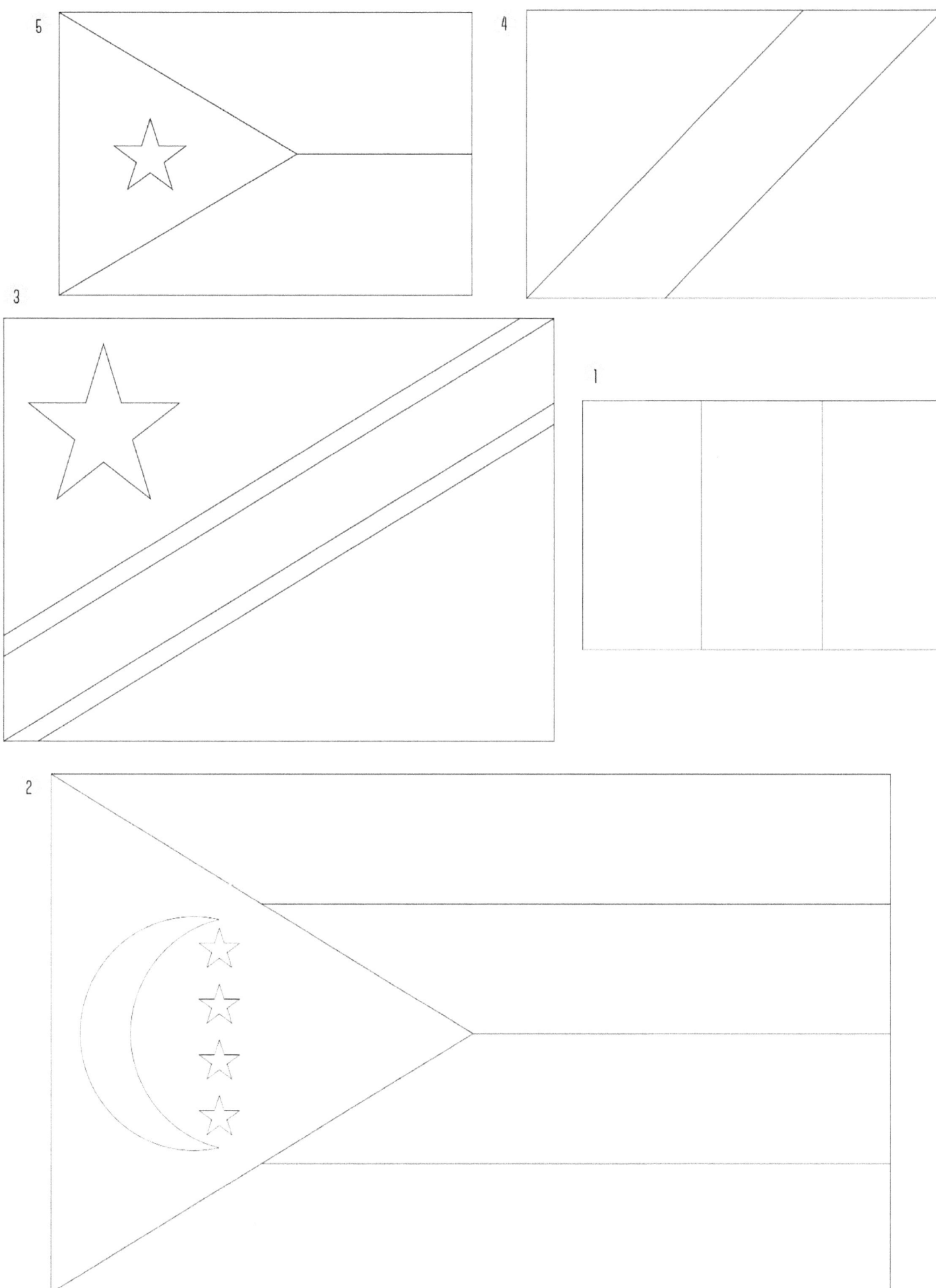

1 FLAG OF EGYPT

3   6   15   16

2 FLAG OF EQUATORIAL GUINEA

3   9   12   16   *EXCLUDING COAT OF ARMS

1

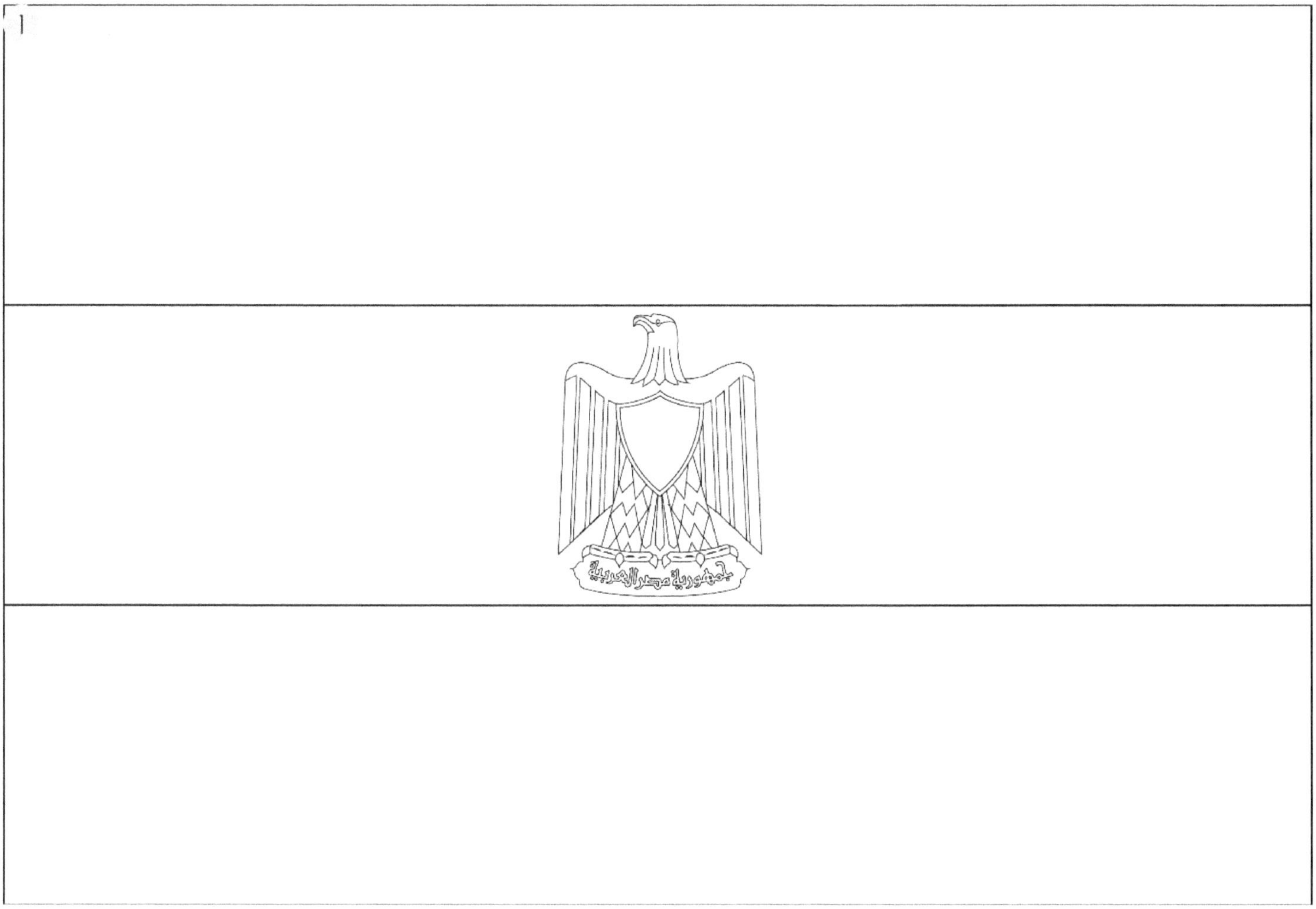

جمهورية مصر العربية

2

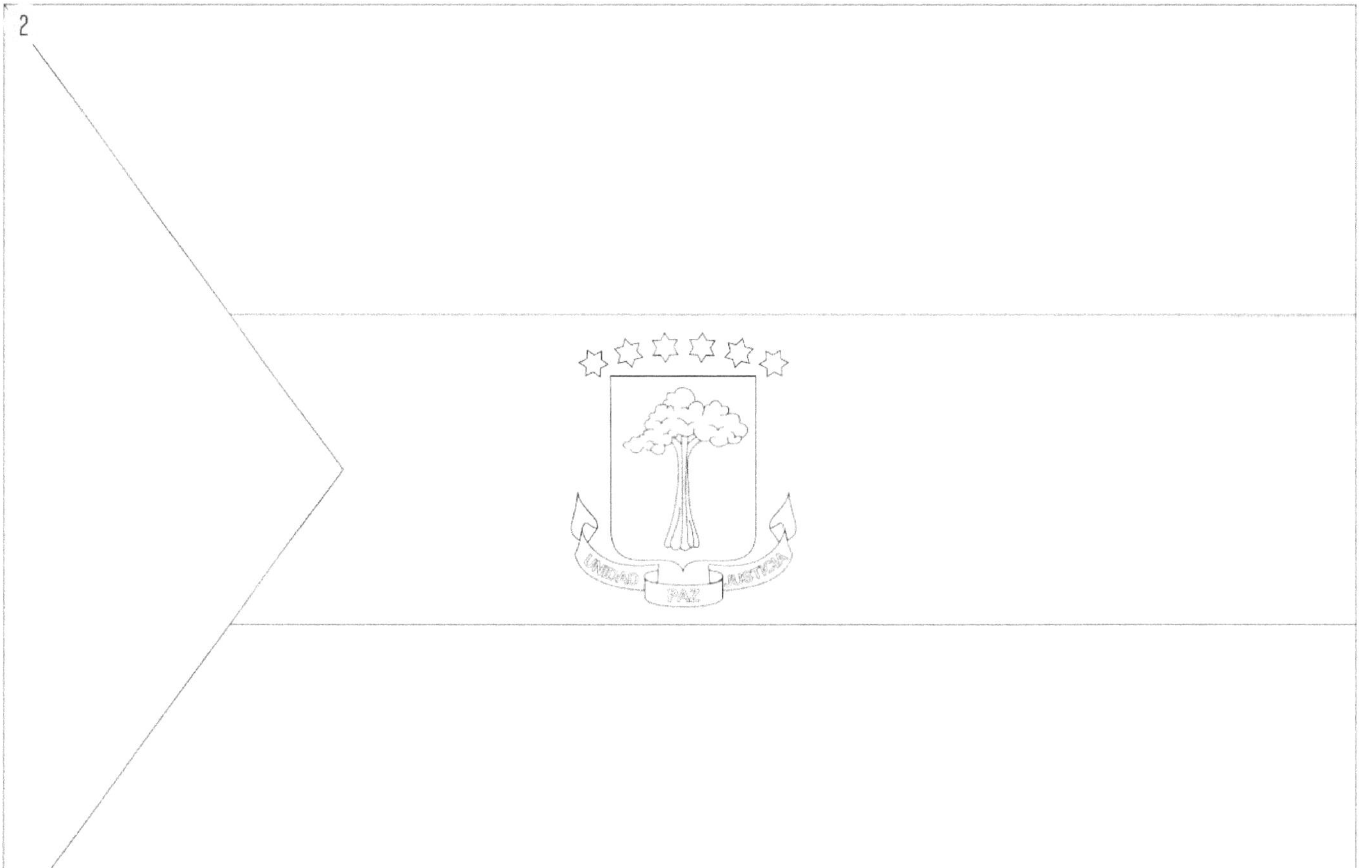

UNIDAD PAZ JUSTICA

1 FLAG OF ERITREA

3　　6　　9　　12

2 FLAG OF ESWATINI

1　　6　　13　　15　　16

1

2

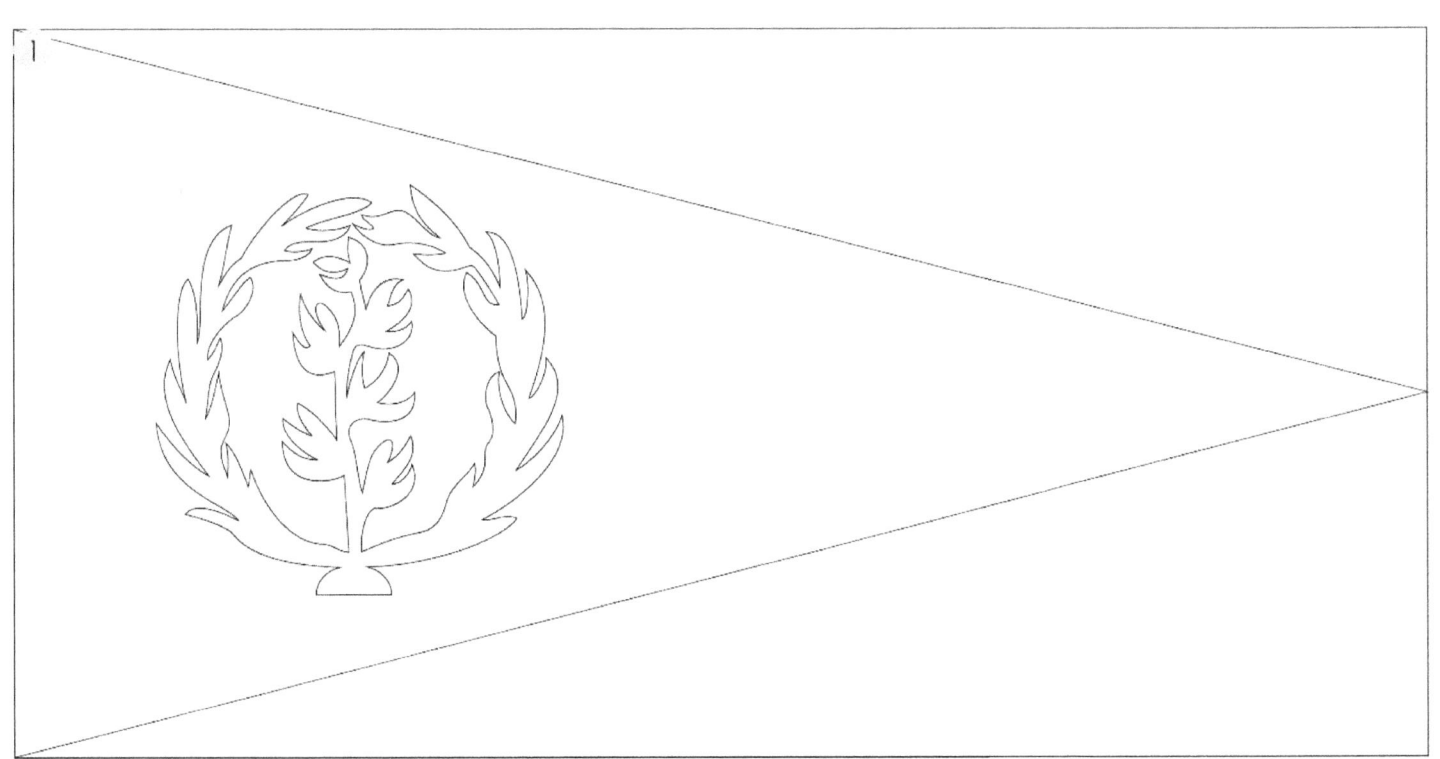

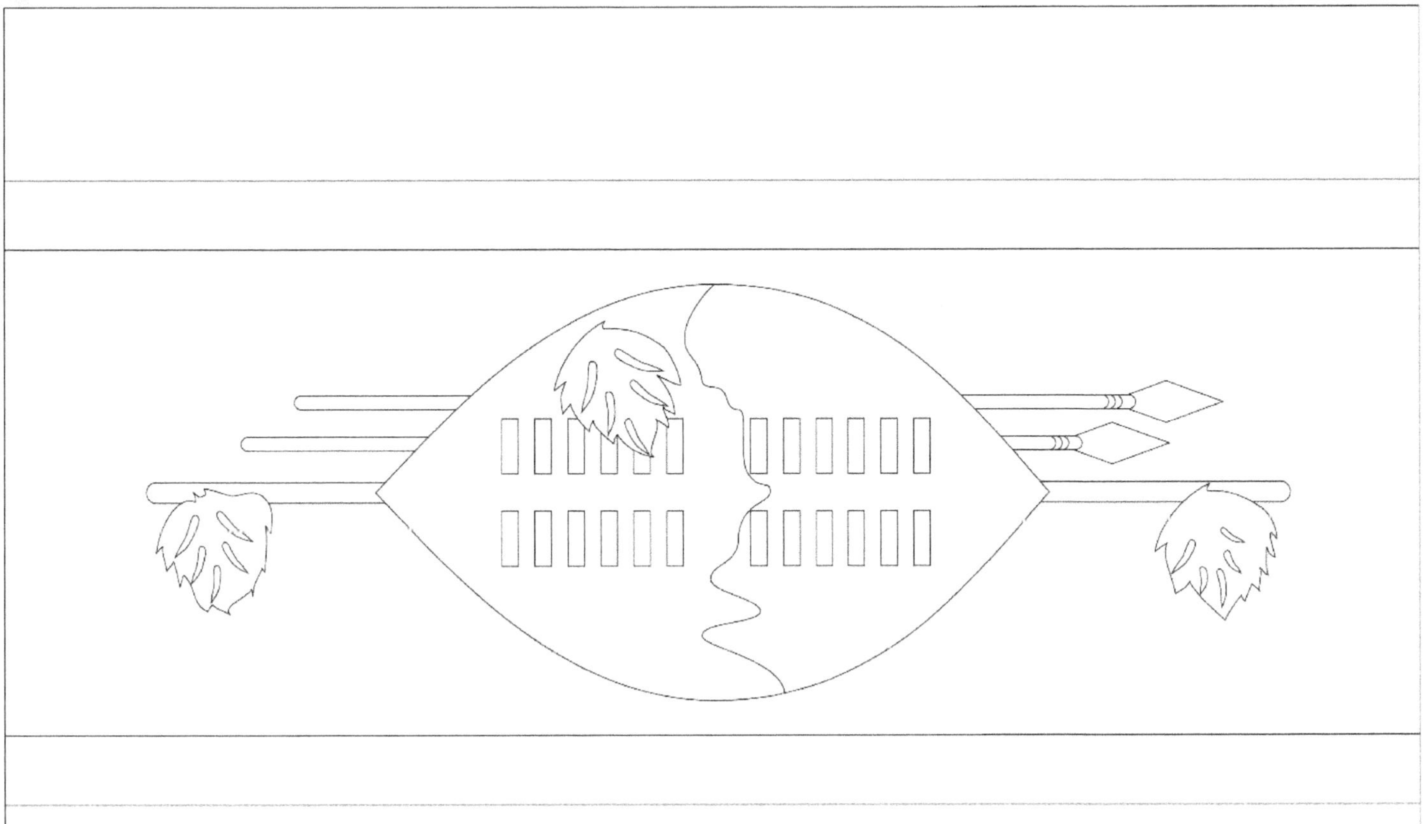

1 FLAG OF ETHIOPIA

3   6   9   13

2 FLAG OF GABON

6   8   12

3 FLAG OF THE GAMBIA

2   10   14   16

4 FLAG OF GHANA

2   6   10   15

5 FLAG OF GUINEA

2   6   9

1 FLAG OF GUINEA-BISSAU
2   6   9   15

2 FLAG OF IVORY COAST
5   9   16

3 FLAG OF KENYA
2   10   15   16

4 FLAG OF LESOTHO
9   14   15   16

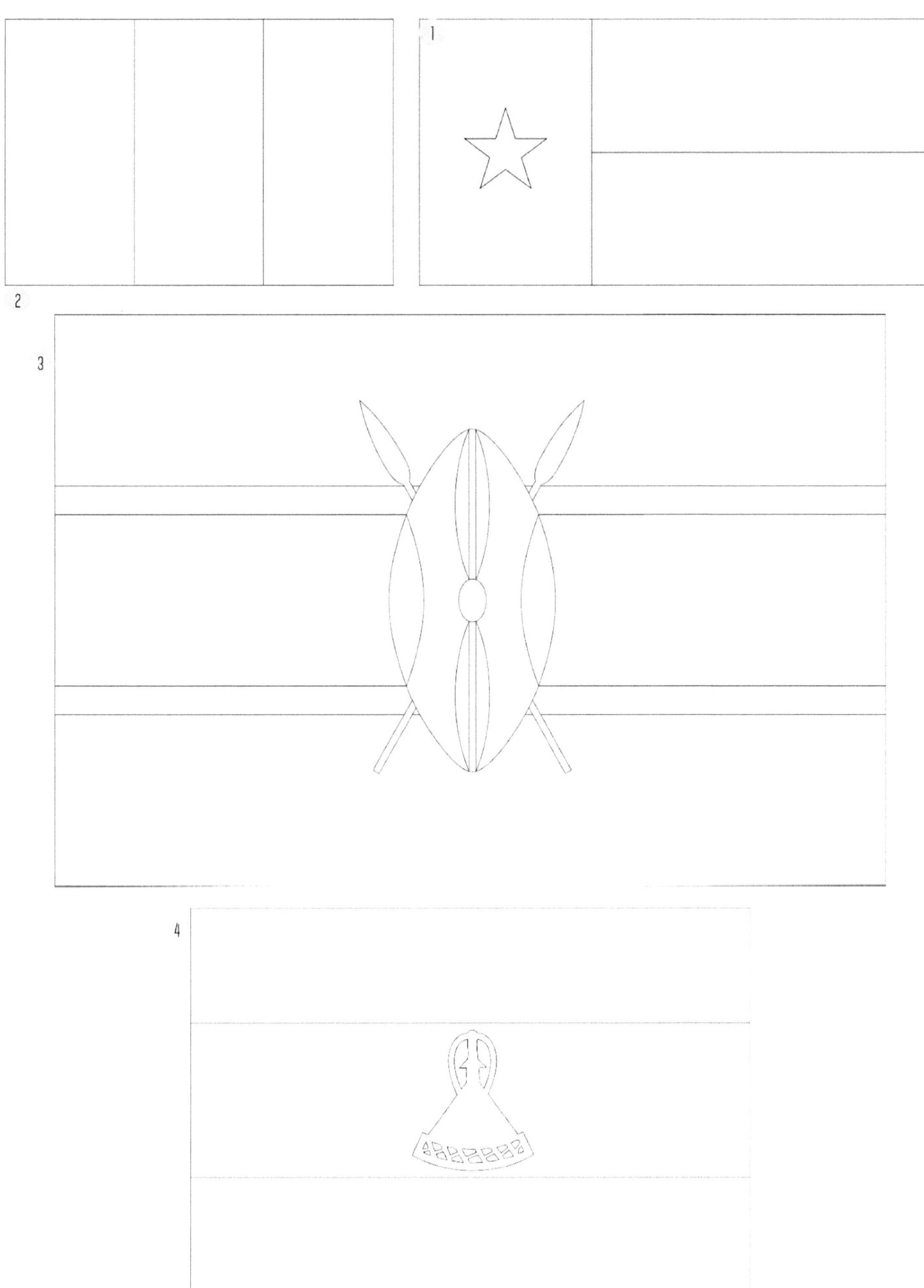

2

3

4

1 FLAG OF LIBERIA

2   14   16

2 FLAG OF LIBYA

3   9   15   16

3 FLAG OF MADAGASCAR

3   10   16

4 FLAG OF MALAWI

2   9   15

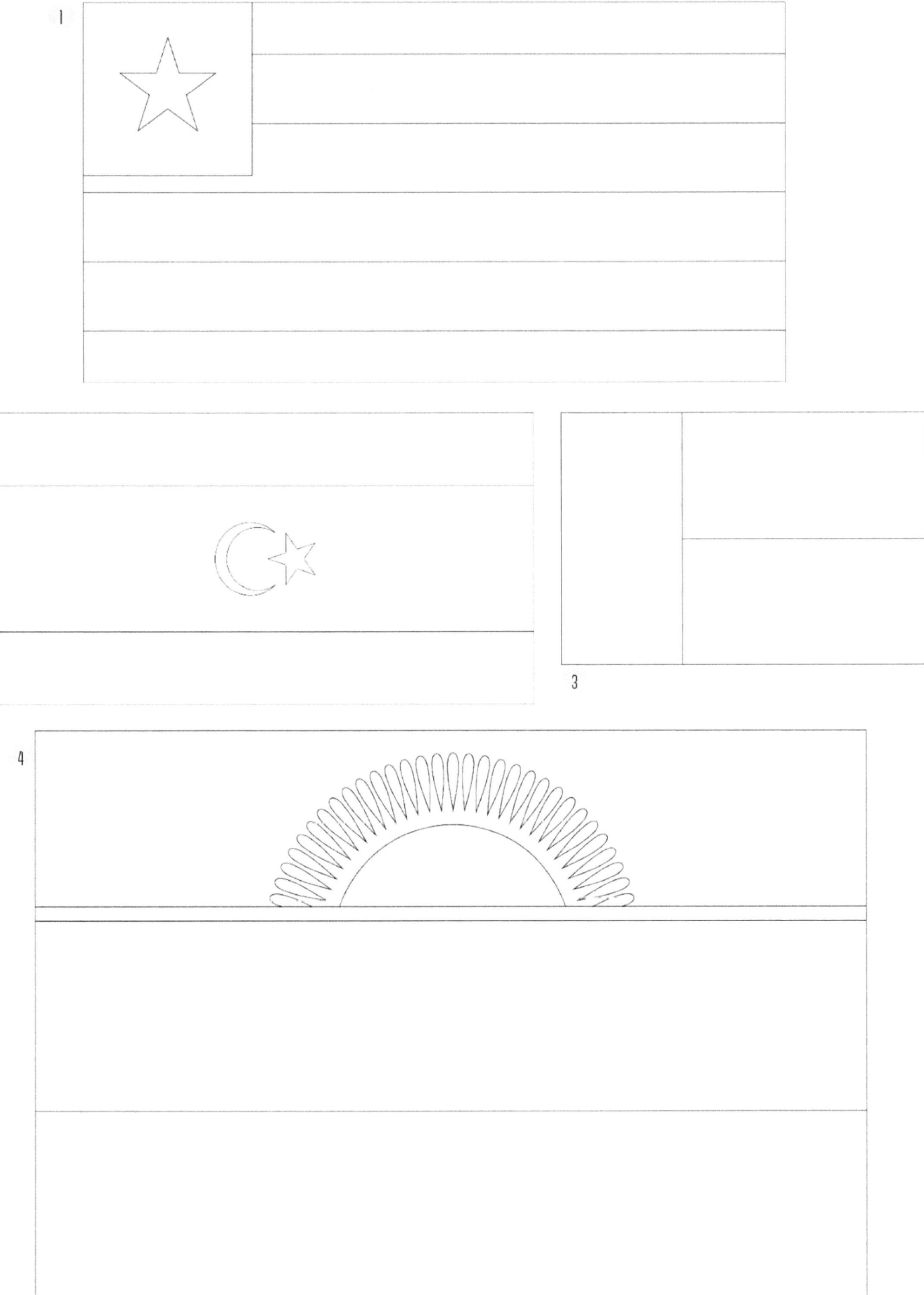

1. FLAG OF MALI
   2   6   8

2. FLAG OF MAURITANIA
   2   6   10

3. FLAG OF MAURITIUS
   3   6   9   14

4. FLAG OF MOROCCO
   2   10

5. FLAG OF MOZAMBIQUE
   3   7   10   15   16

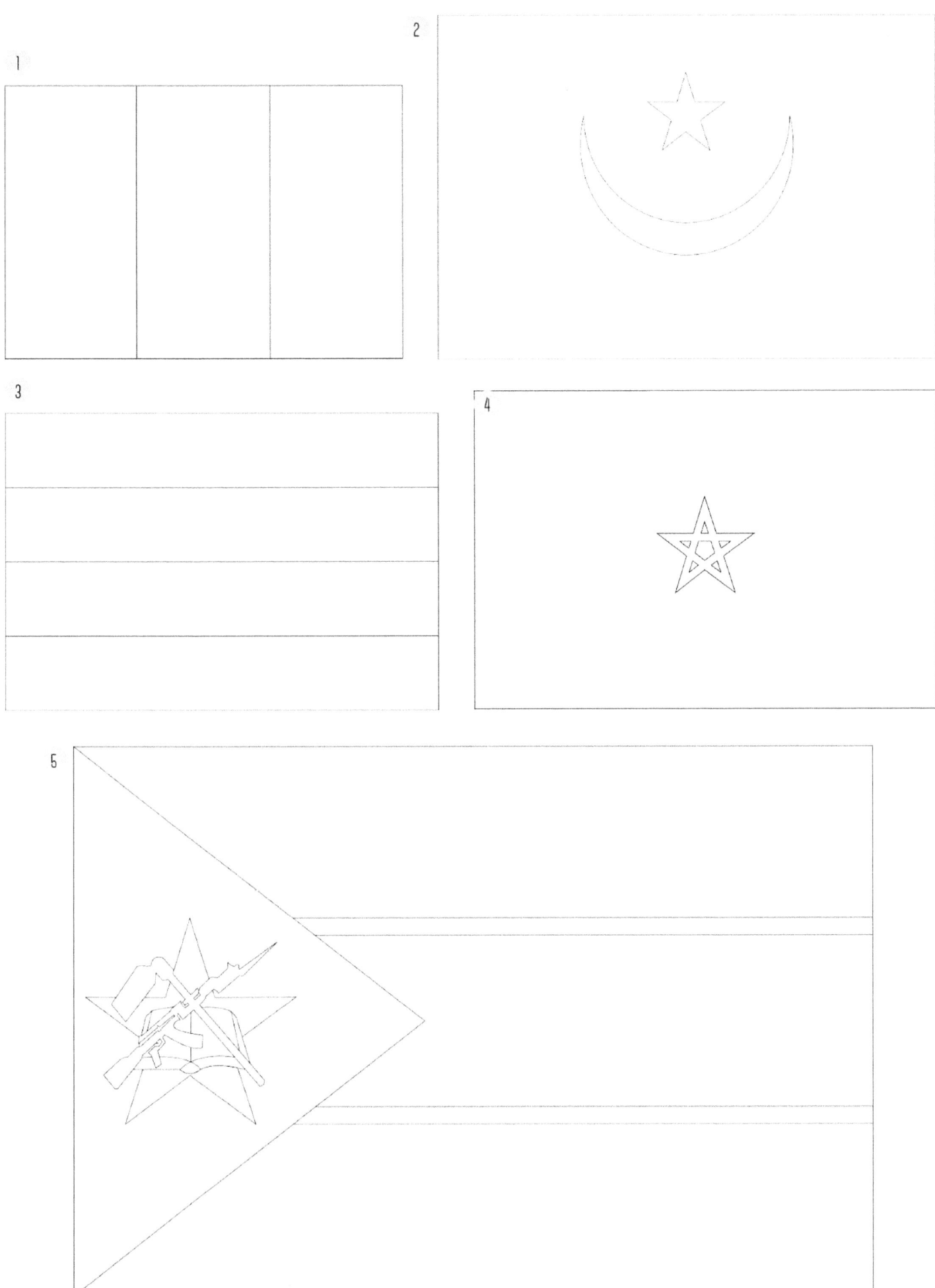

1 FLAG OF NAMIBIA

2   6   9   14   16

2 FLAG OF NIGER

4   9   16

3 FLAG OF NIGERIA

9   16

4 FLAG OF RWANDA

6   10   12

1 FLAG OF SAO TOME AND PRINCIPE

2   6   8   15

2 FLAG OF SENEGAL

3   6   9

3 FLAG OF SEYCHELLES

3   7   10   14   16

4 FLAG OF SIERRA LEONE

8   12   16

5 FLAG OF SOMALIA

12   16

1 FLAG OF SOUTH AFRICA

    3   6   10   14   15   16

2 FLAG OF SOUTH SUDAN

    3   7   9   13   15   16

3 FLAG OF SUDAN

    2   9   15   16

4 FLAG OF TANZANIA

    6   8   12   15

5 FLAG OF TOGO

    2   6   10   16

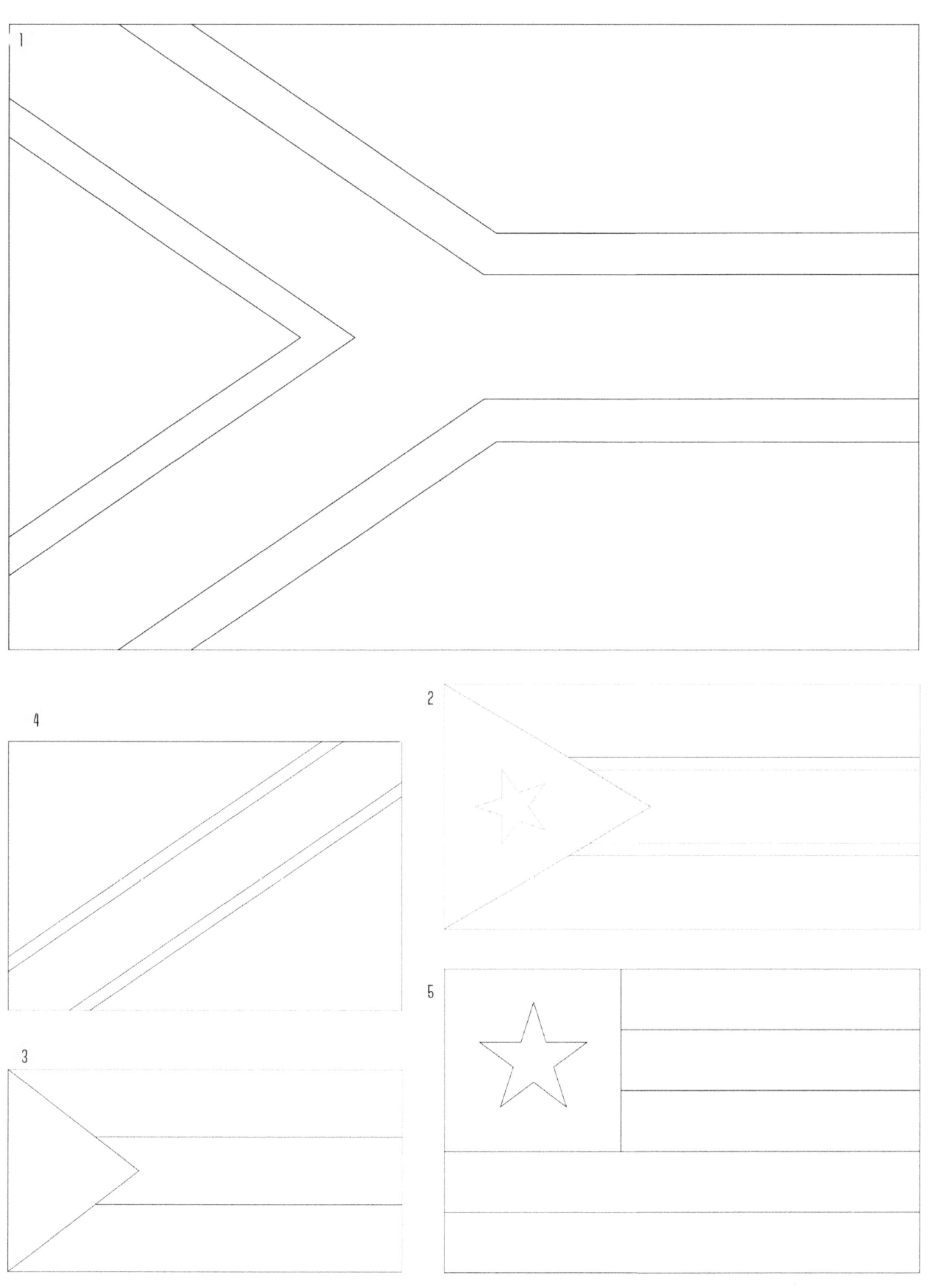

1 FLAG OF TUNISIA

3   16

2 FLAG OF UGANDA

3   7   15   16   *EXCLUDING COAT OF ARMS

3 FLAG OF ZAMBIA

3   5   9   15

4 FLAG OF ZIMBABWE

2   6   10   15   16

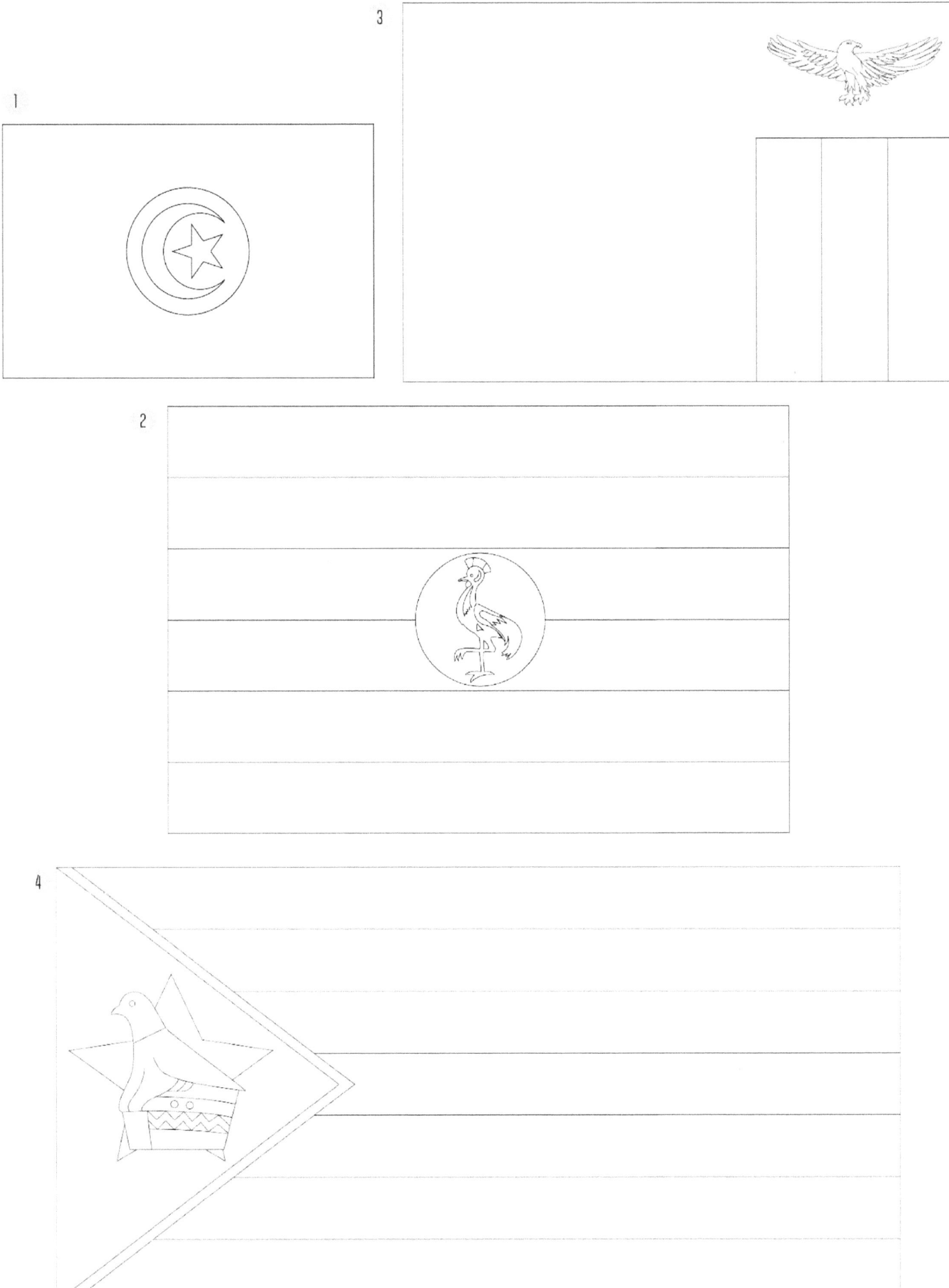

FLAGS OF EUROPE
A-Z

1 FLAG OF ALBANIA

3   15

2 FLAG OF ANDORRA

2   6   14   *EXCLUDING COAT OF ARMS

3 FLAG OF AUSTRIA

3   16

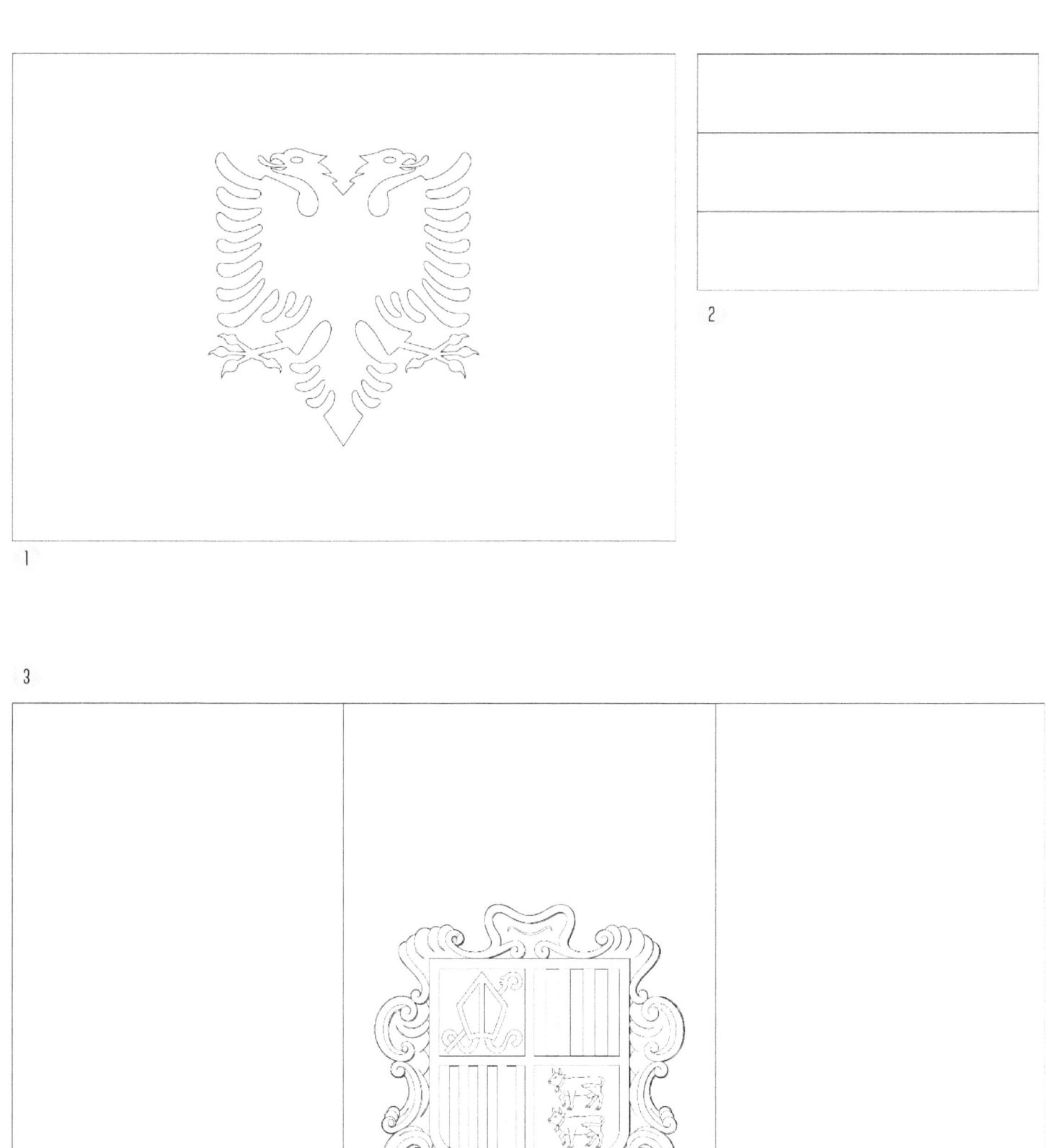

1

2

3

VIRTVS VNITA FORTIOR

1

2

4

3

1 FLAG OF CROATIA

3   14   16   *EXCLUDING COAT OF ARMS

2 FLAG OF CYPRUS

5   10   16

3 FLAG OF CZECH REPUBLIC

3   14   16

4 FLAG OF DENMARK

2   16

5 FLAG OF ESTONIA

13   15   16

6 FLAG OF FINLAND

14   16

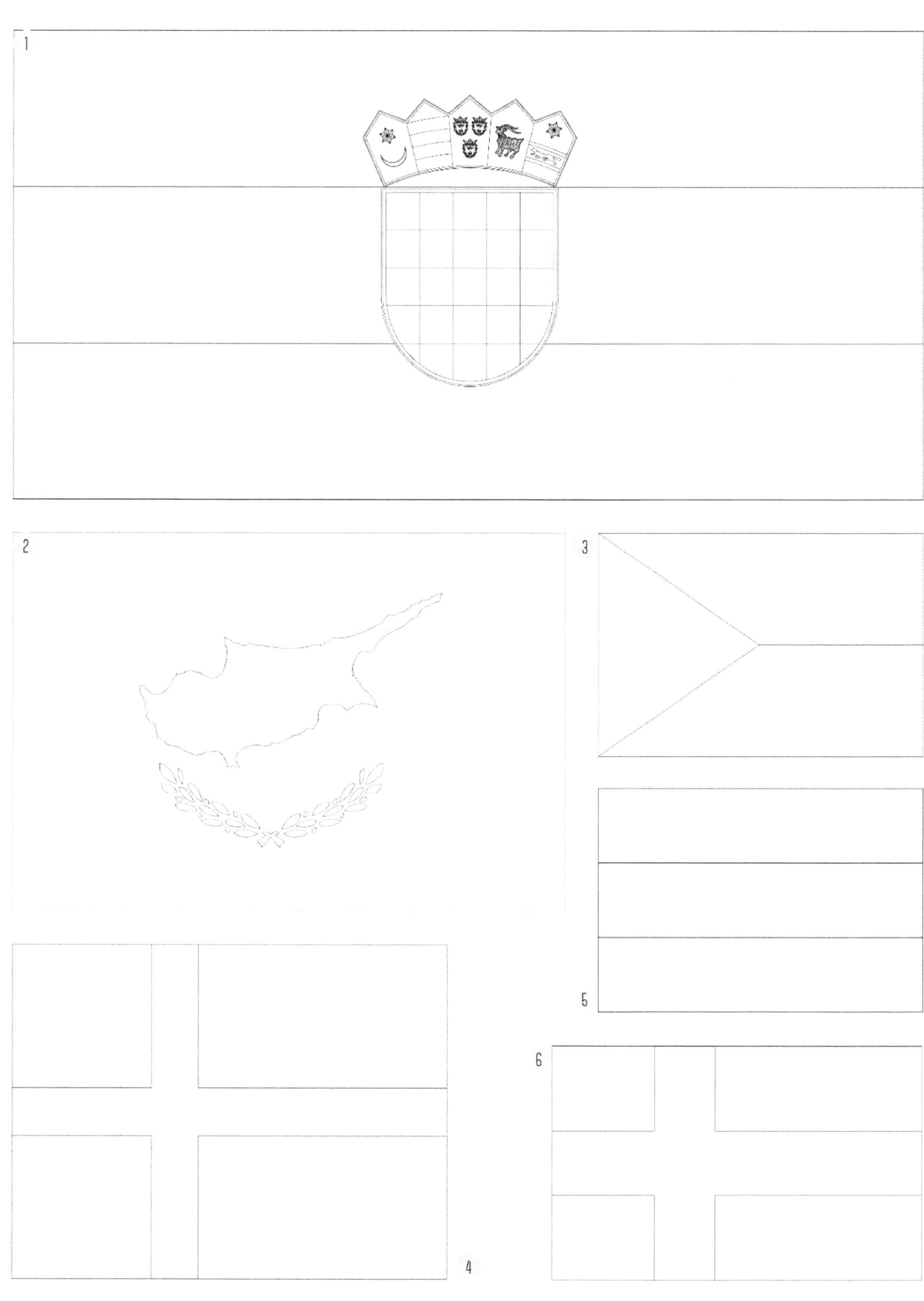

1 FLAG OF FRANCE
3   14   16

2 FLAG OF GERMANY
3   6   15

3 FLAG OF GREECE
13   16

4 FLAG OF HUNGARY
2   10   16

5 FLAG OF ICELAND
3   13   16

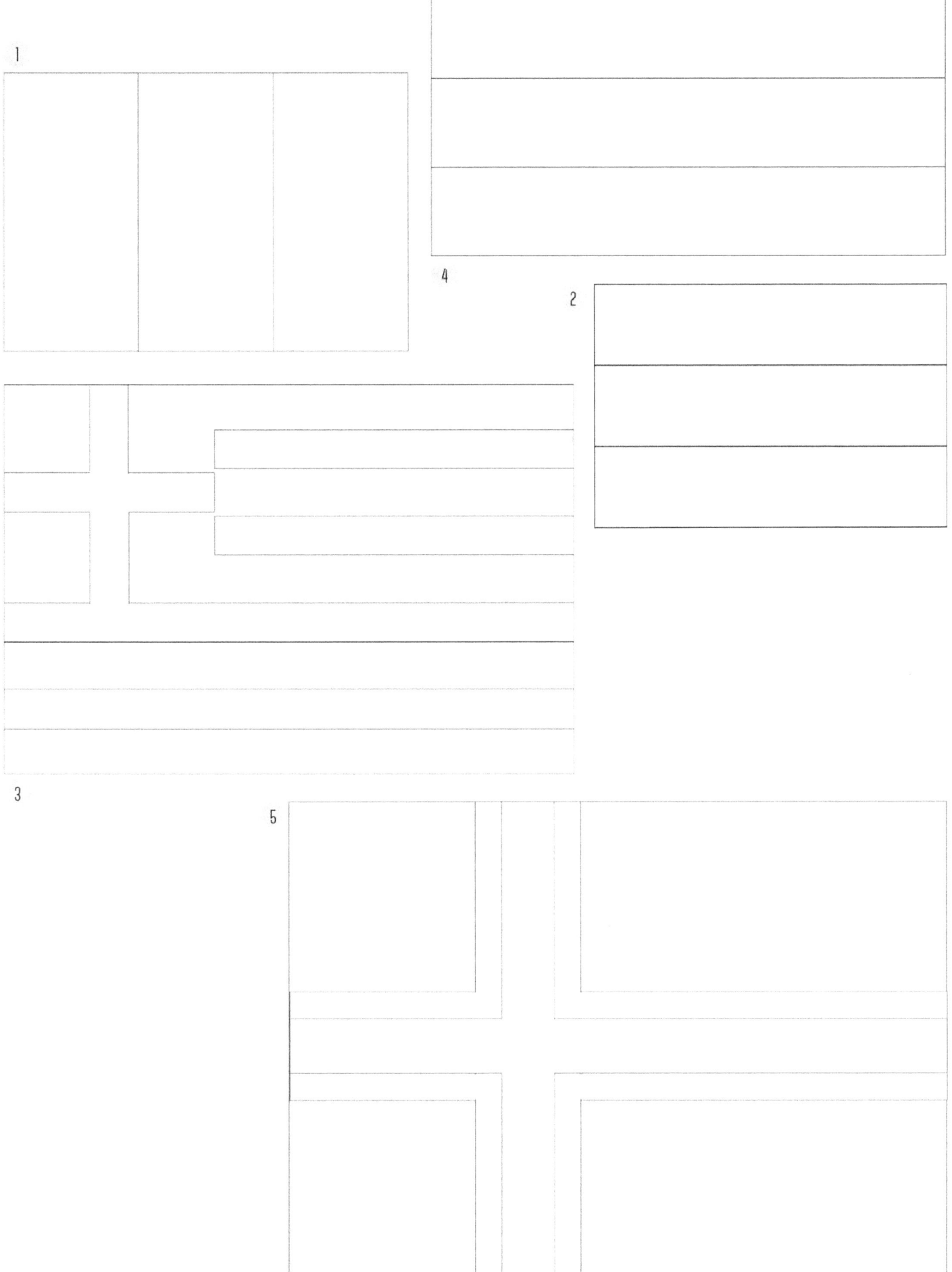

1 FLAG OF IRELAND

5   9   16

2 FLAG OF ITALY

2   9   16

3 FLAG OF KOSOVO

6   14   16

4 FLAG OF LATVIA

1   16

5 FLAG OF LIECHTENSTEIN

2   6   14   16

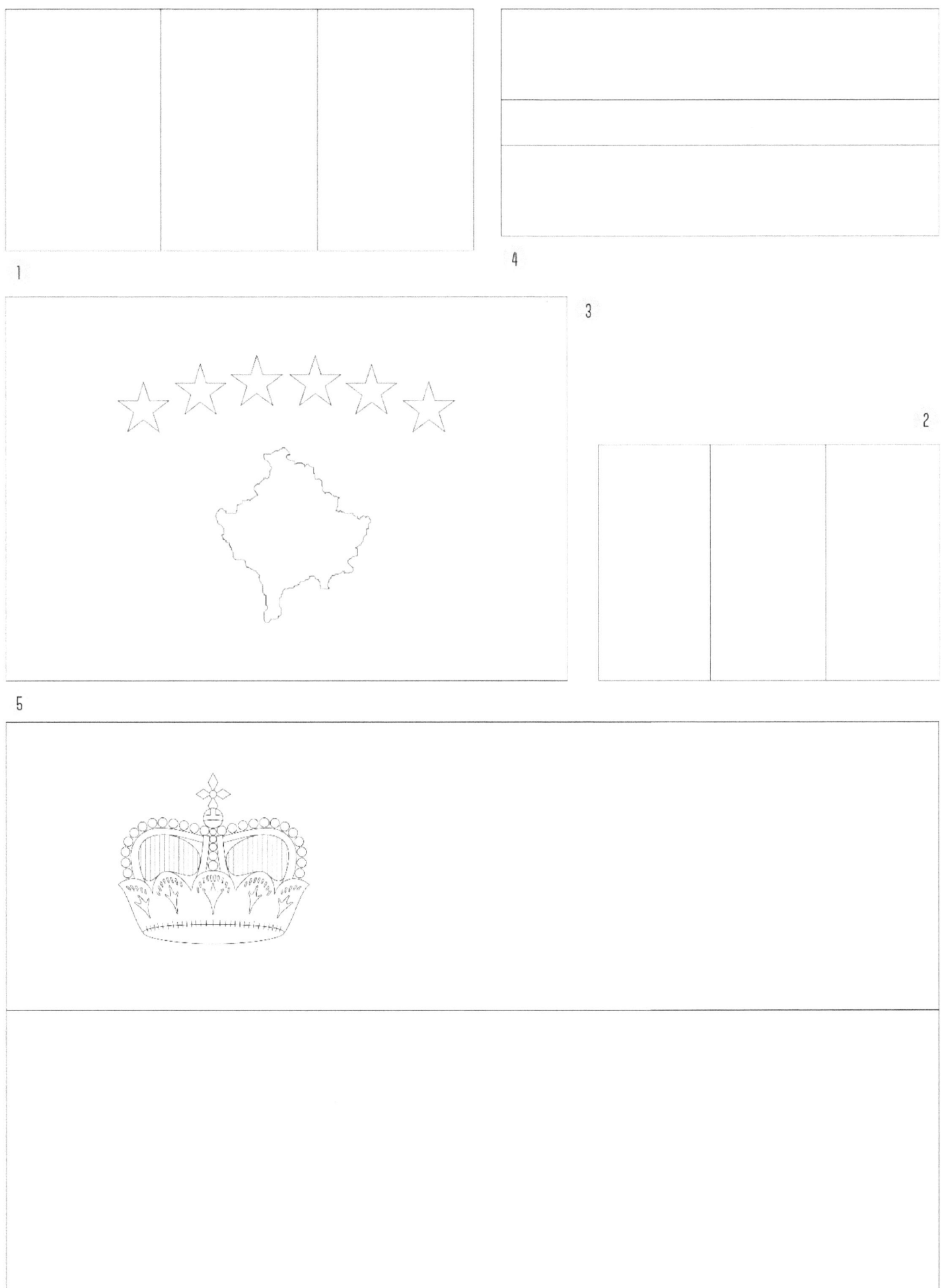

1

4

3

2

5

1 FLAG OF LITHUANIA

2   6   10

2 FLAG OF LUXEMBOURG

3   12   16

3 FLAG OF MALTA

2   16   *EXCLUDING COAT OF ARMS

4 FLAG OF MOLDOVA

2   6   13   *EXCLUDING COAT OF ARMS

5 FLAG OF MONACO

2   16

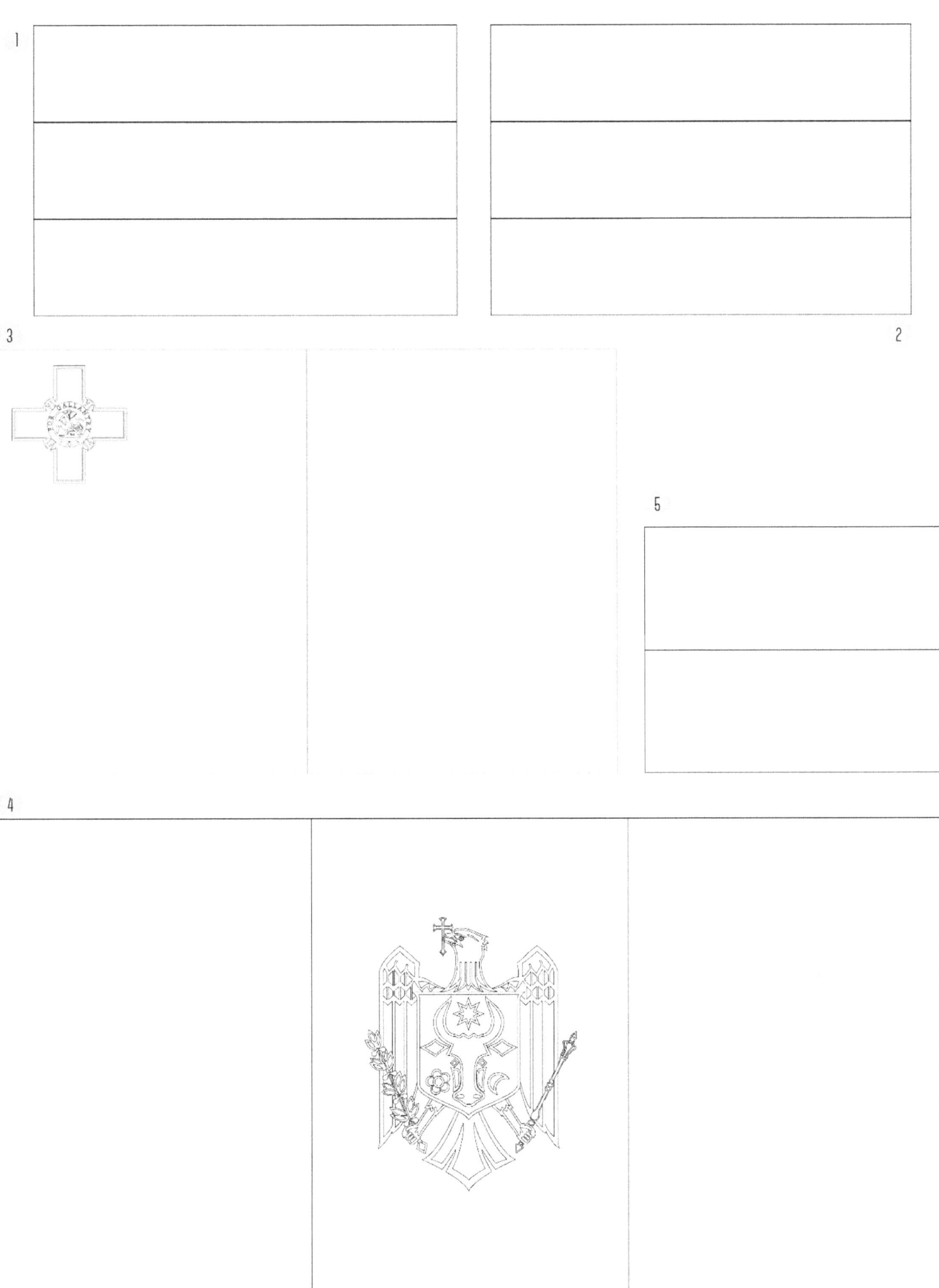

1 FLAG OF MONTENEGRO

2   6   *EXCLUDING COAT OF ARMS

2 FLAG OF THE NETHERLANDS

2   14   16

3 FLAG OF NORTH MACEDONIA

2   7

4 FLAG OF NORWAY

3   14   16

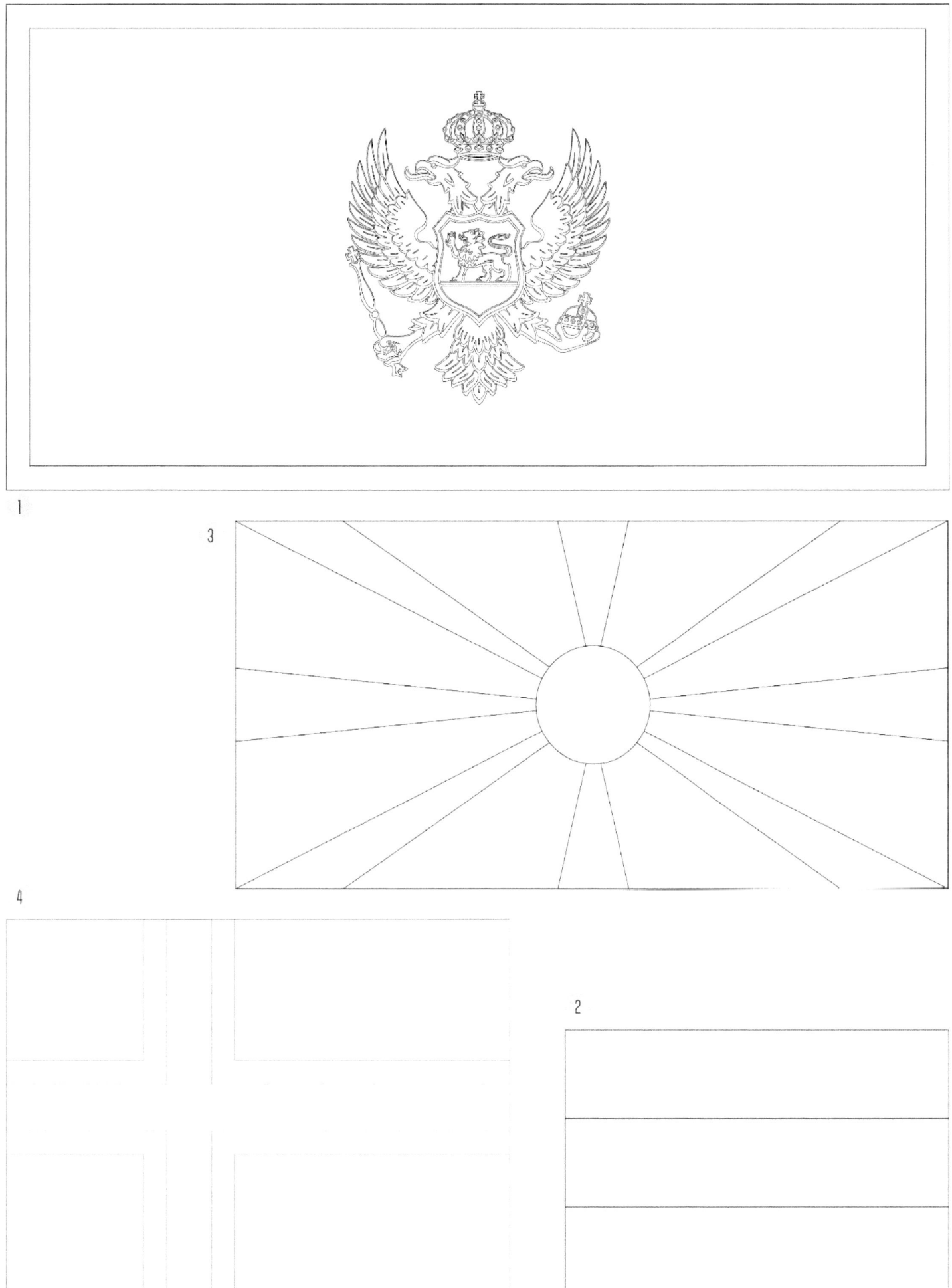

1

3

4

2

① FLAG OF POLAND
2   16

② FLAG OF PORTUGAL
3   7   10   *EXCLUDING COAT OF ARMS

③ FLAG OF ROMANIA
2   6   14

④ FLAG OF RUSSIA
2   14   16

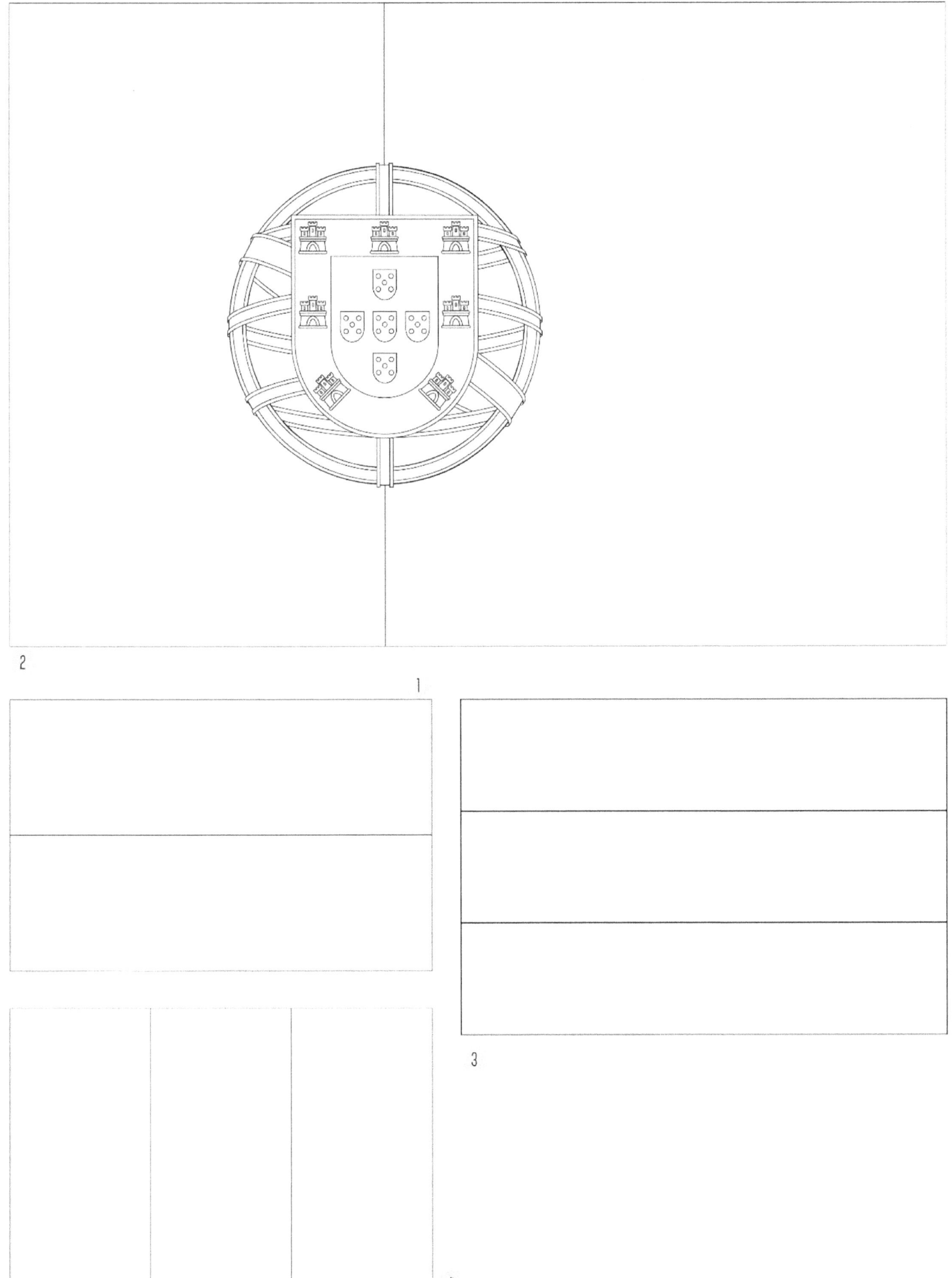

2

1

3

4

① FLAG OF SAN MARINO

11   16   *EXCLUDING COAT OF ARMS

② FLAG OF SERBIA

2   14   16   *EXCLUDING COAT OF ARMS

1

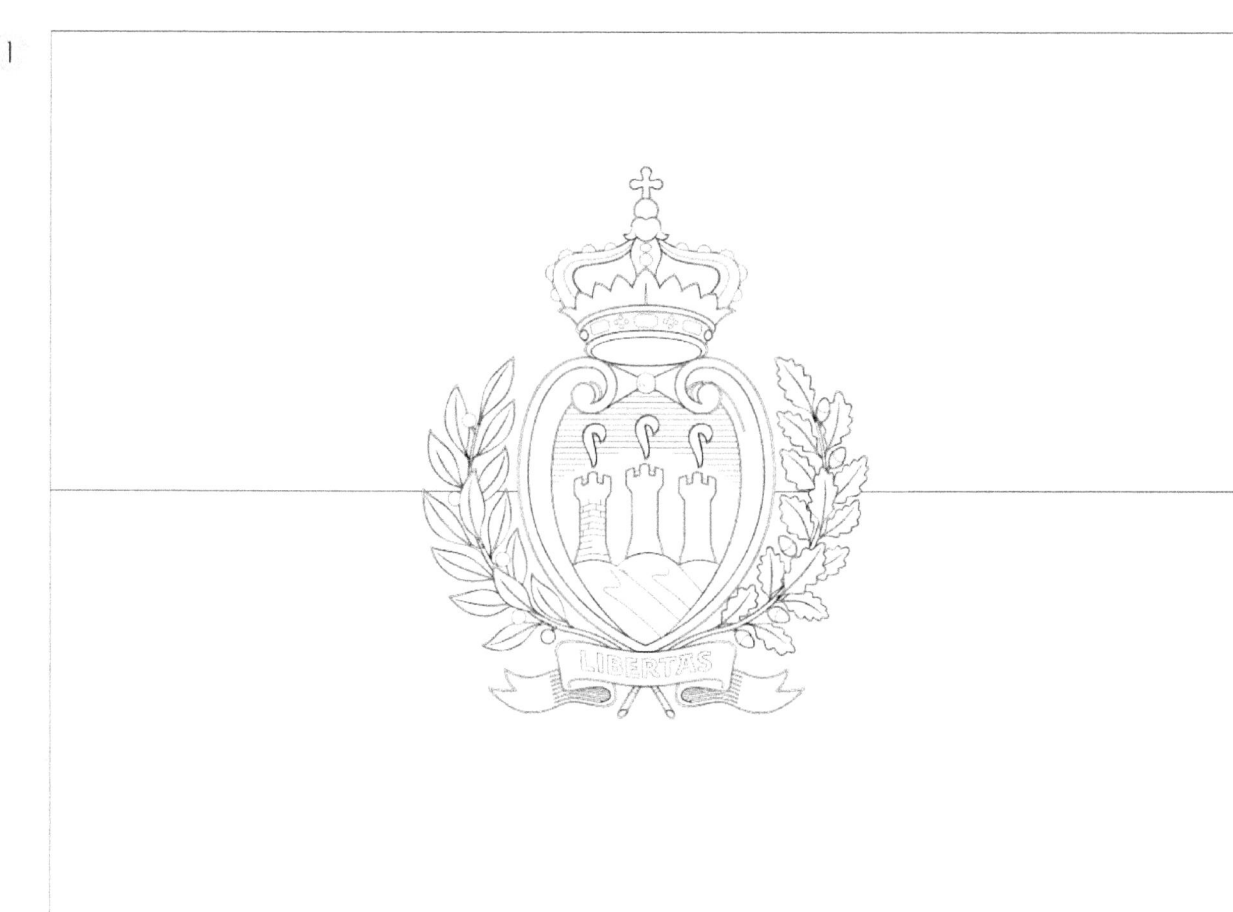

2

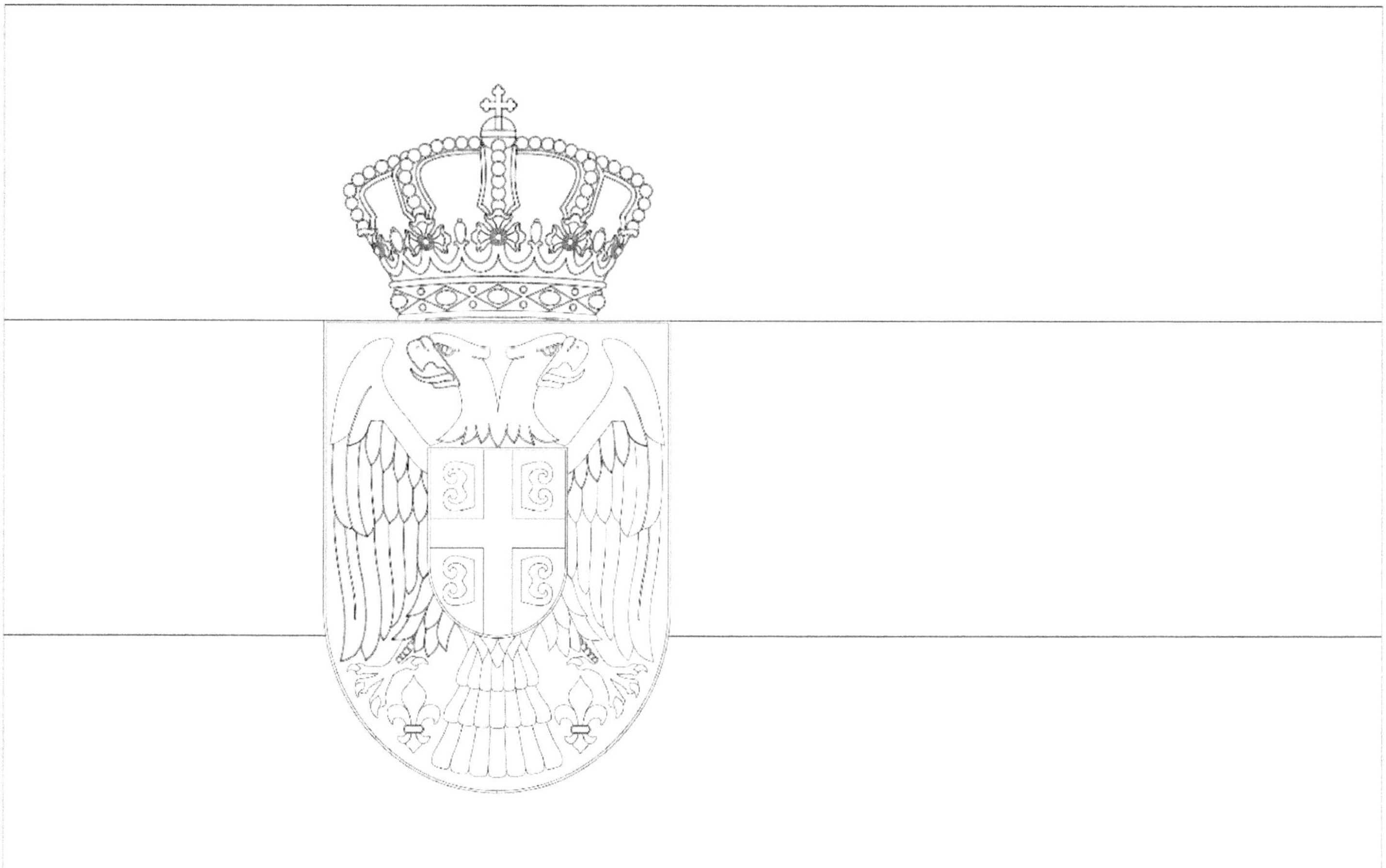

① FLAG OF SLOVAKIA

3   14   16

② FLAG OF SLOVENIA

3   7   13   16

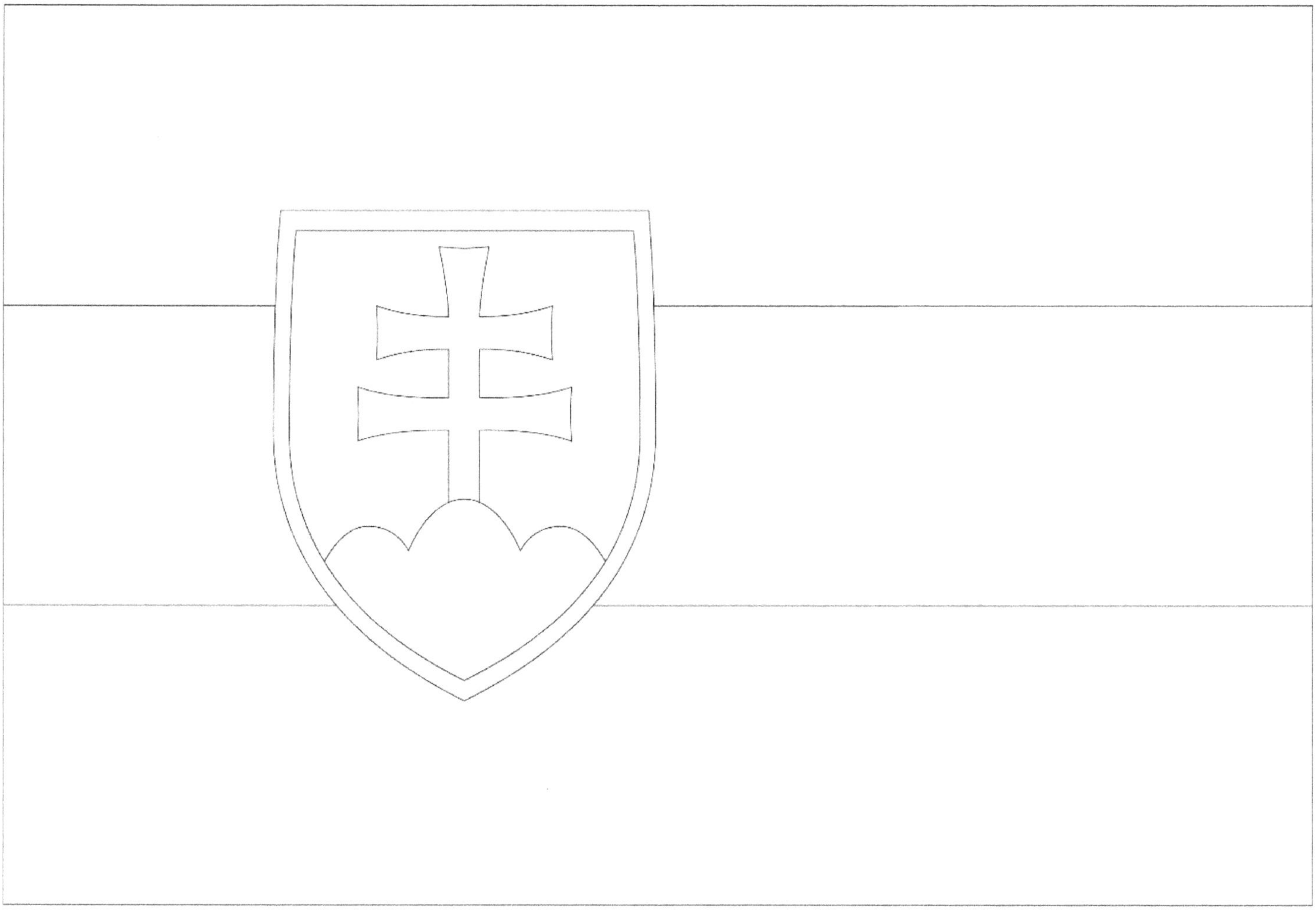

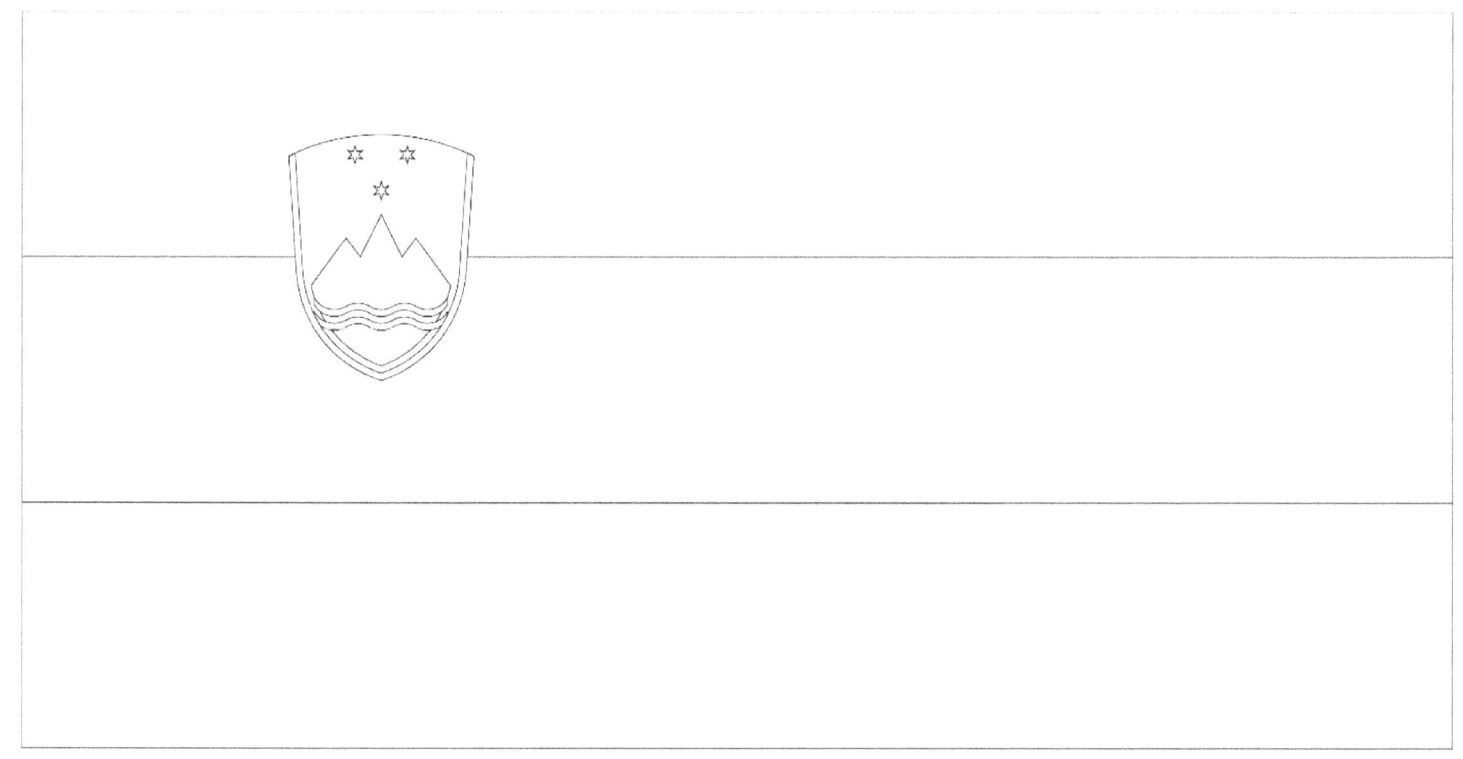

1

2

1 FLAG OF SPAIN

2   6   *EXCLUDING COAT OF ARMS

2 FLAG OF SWEDEN

6   13

3 FLAG OF SWITZERLAND

3   16

4 FLAG OF UKRAINE

7   13

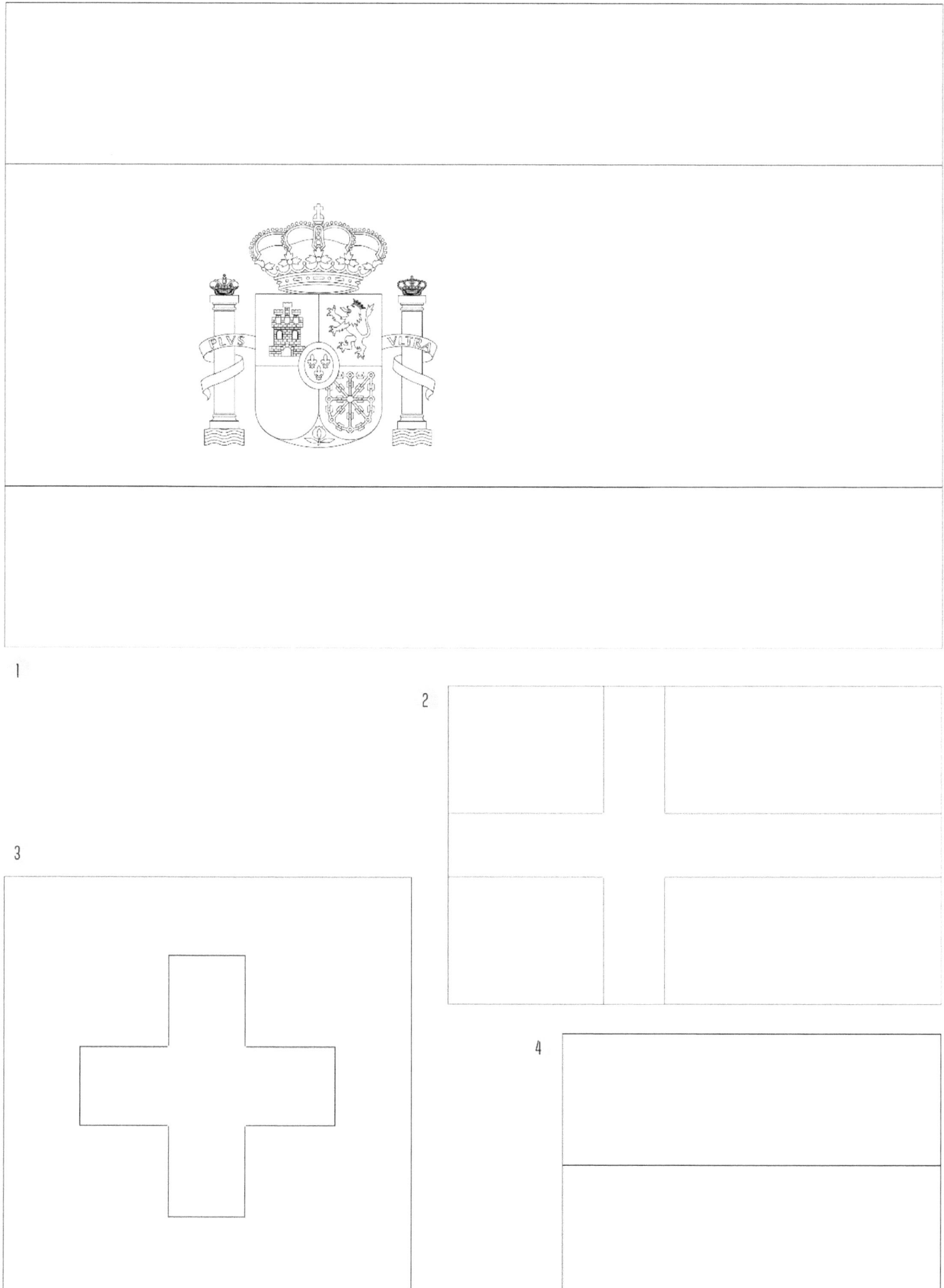

1

2

3

4

FLAG OF THE UNITED KINGDOM

2   14   16

FLAG OF VATICAN CITY

7   16   *EXCLUDING COAT OF ARMS

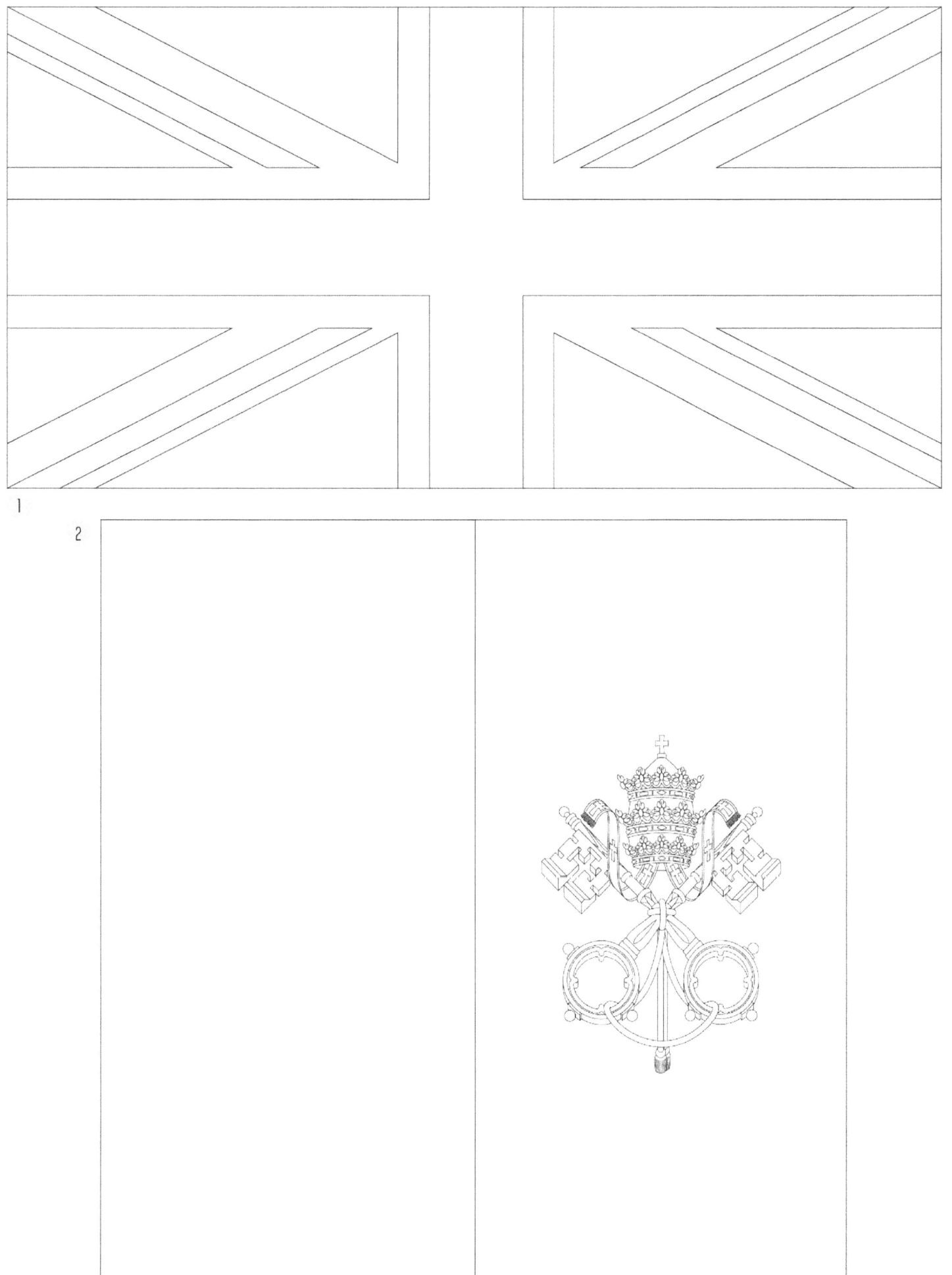

1

2

FLAGS OF ASIA
A-Z

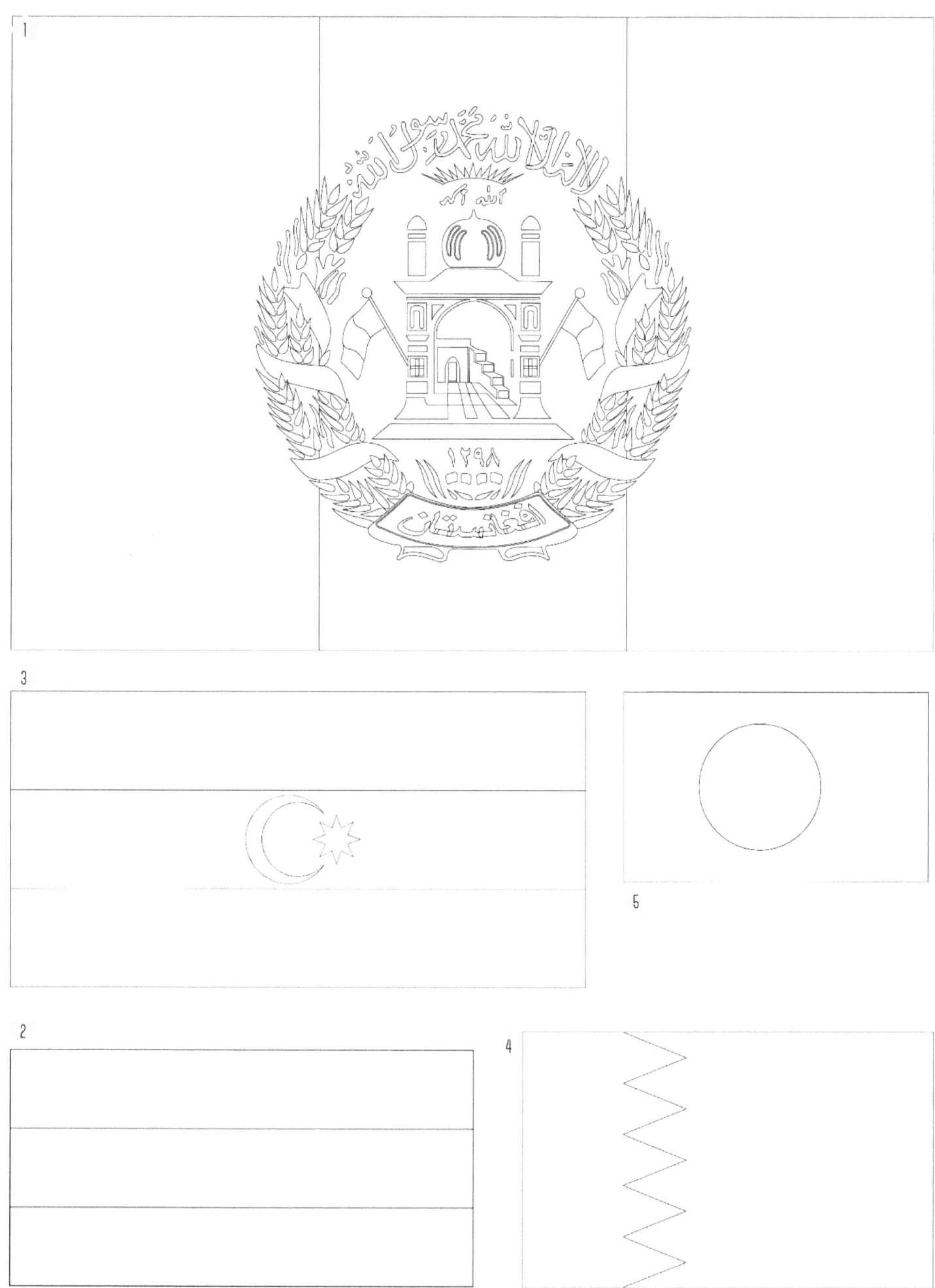

1 FLAG OF BHUTAN

4   6   16

2 FLAG OF BRUNEI

2   7   15   16

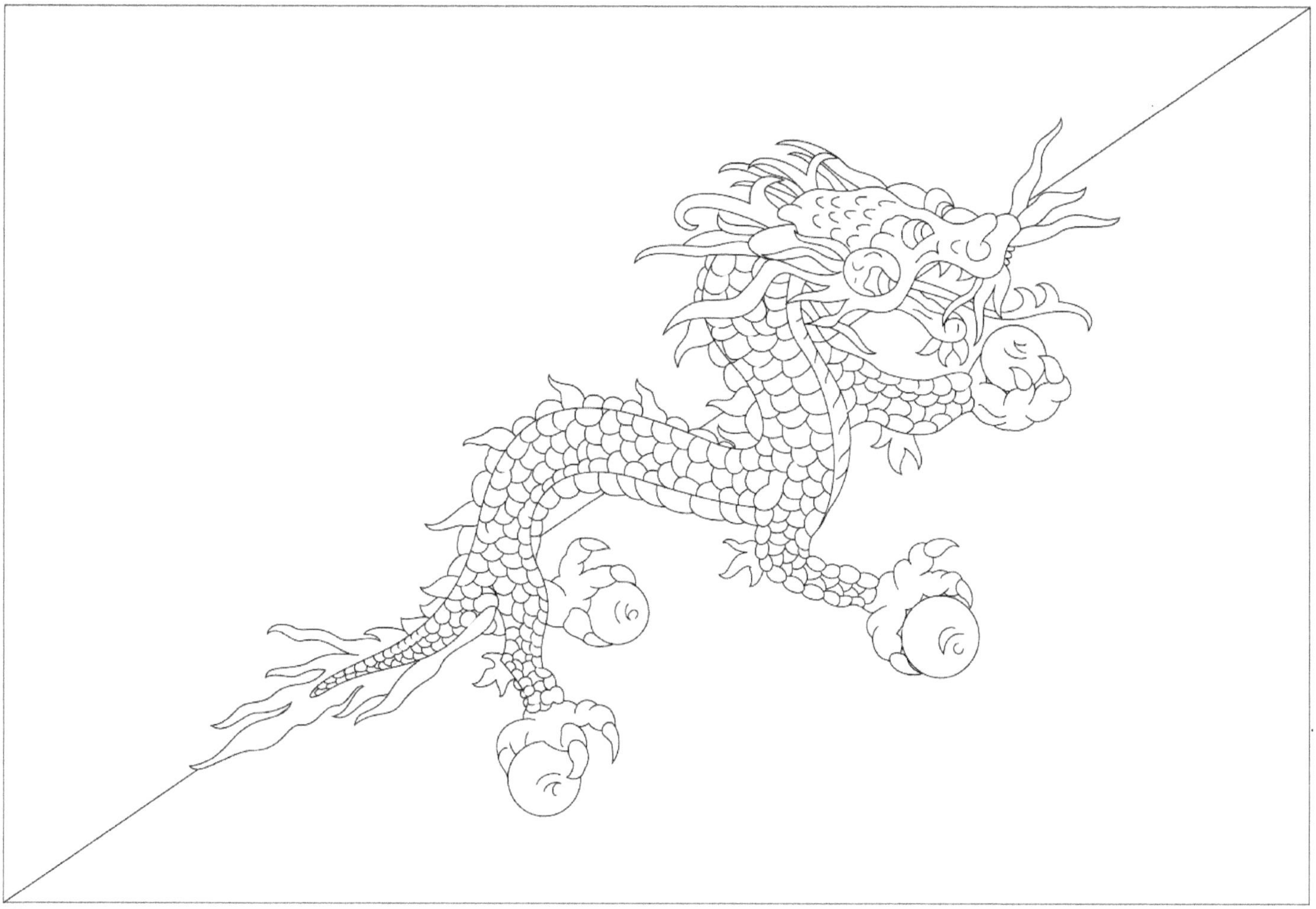

1

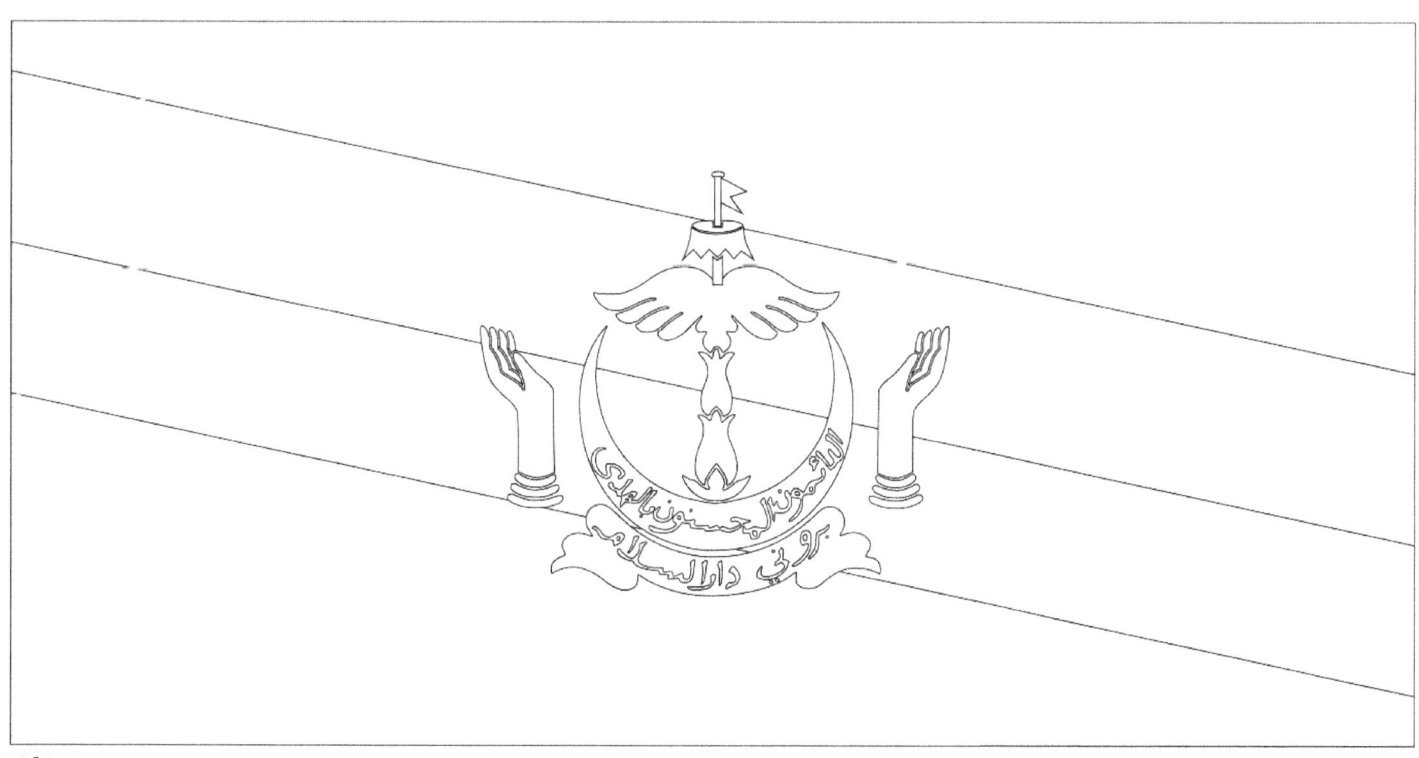

2

1 FLAG OF CAMBODIA

3   14   16

2 FLAG OF CHINA

2   6

3 FLAG OF GEORGIA

3   16

1

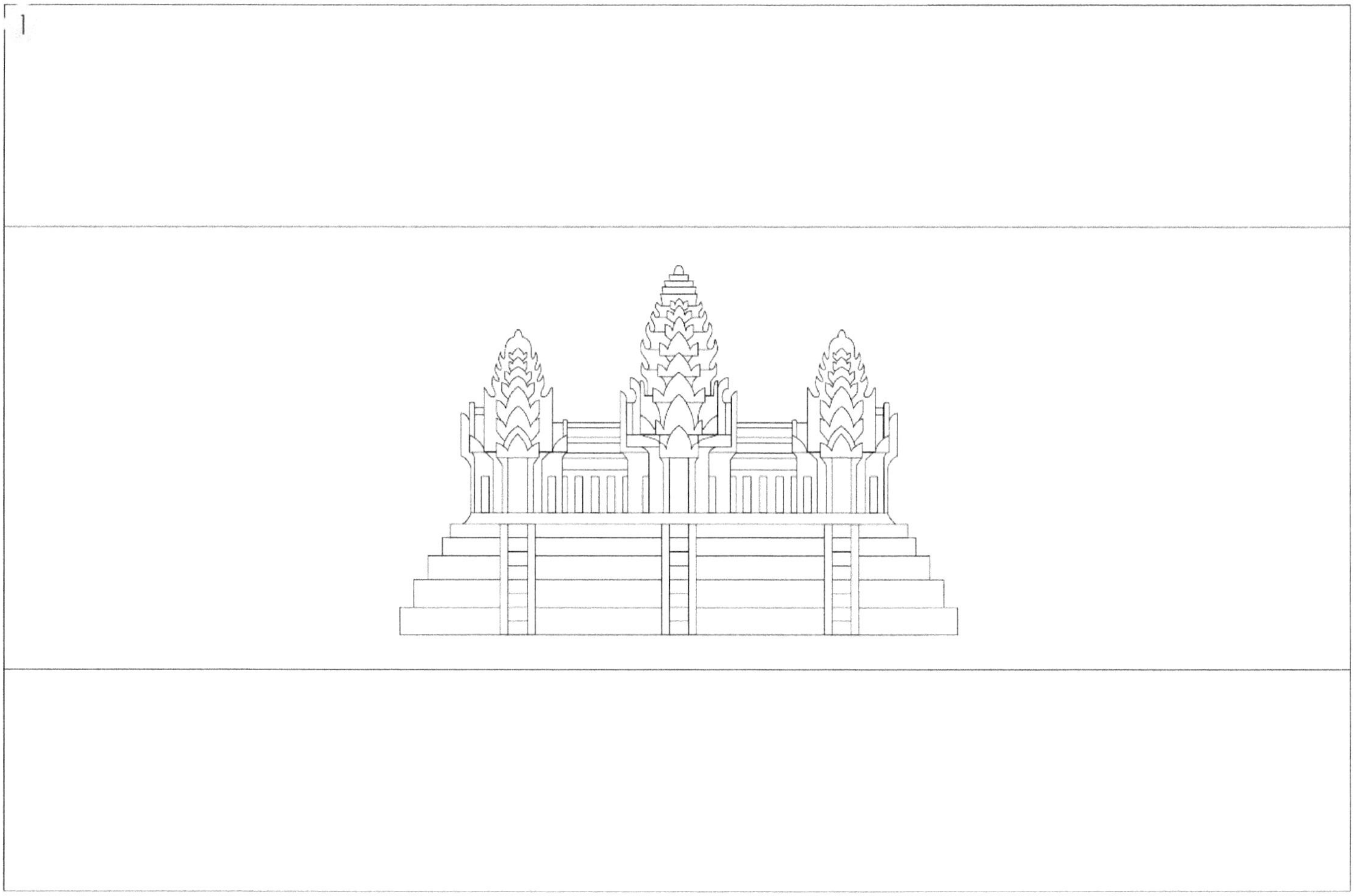

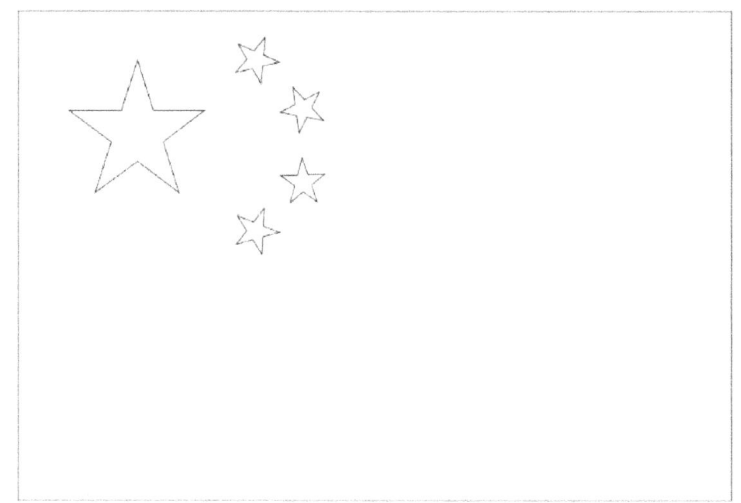

2

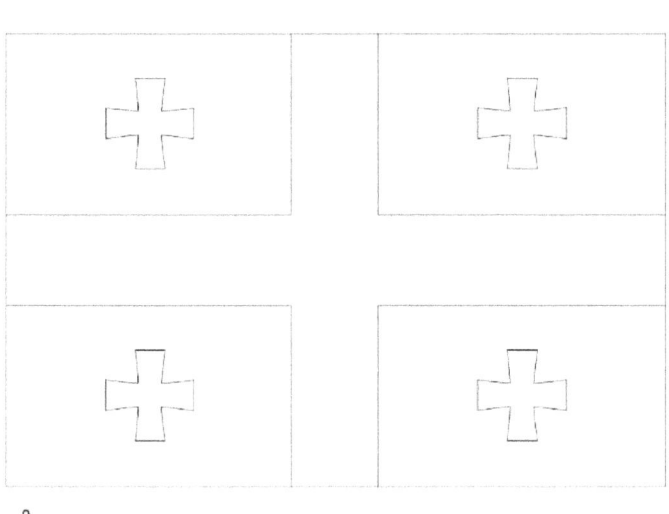

3

1 FLAG OF INDIA

5   9   14   16

2 FLAG OF INDONESIA

3   16

3 FLAG OF IRAN

2   9   16

1

2

3

1 FLAG OF IRAQ
  2   10   15   16

2 FLAG OF ISRAEL
  13   16

3 FLAG OF JAPAN
  2   16

4 FLAG OF JORDAN
  2   10   15   16

5 FLAG OF KAZAKHSTAN
  7   11

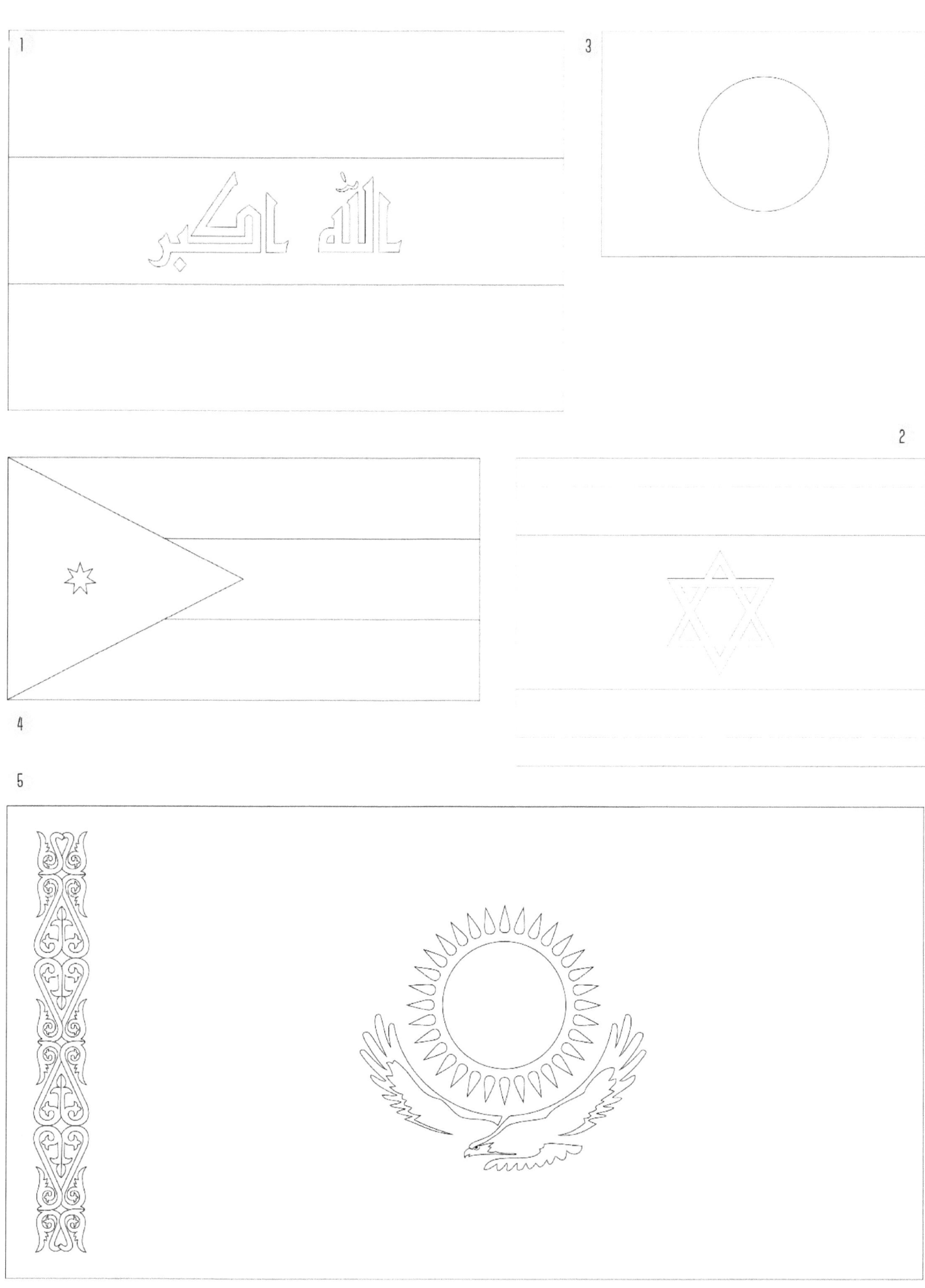

1 FLAG OF KUWAIT
2   10   15   16

2 FLAG OF KYRGYZSTAN
3   7

3 FLAG OF LAOS
2   14   16

4 FLAG OF LEBANON
3   9   16

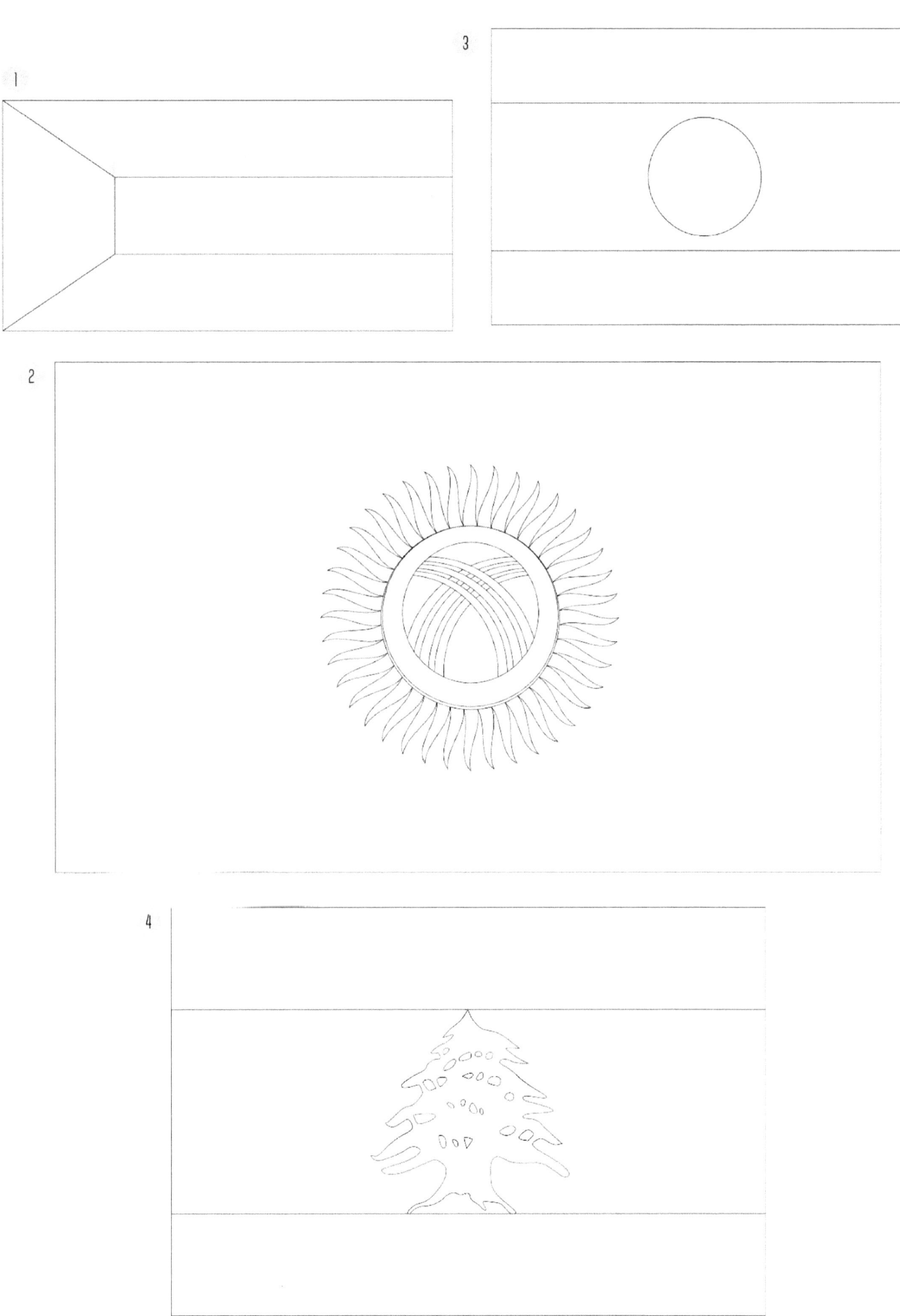

1 FLAG OF MALAYSIA
   2   6   14   16

2 FLAG OF MALDIVES
   2   10   16

3 FLAG OF MONGOLIA
   2   6   13

4 FLAG OF MYANMAR
   2   6   8   16

1

3

2

4

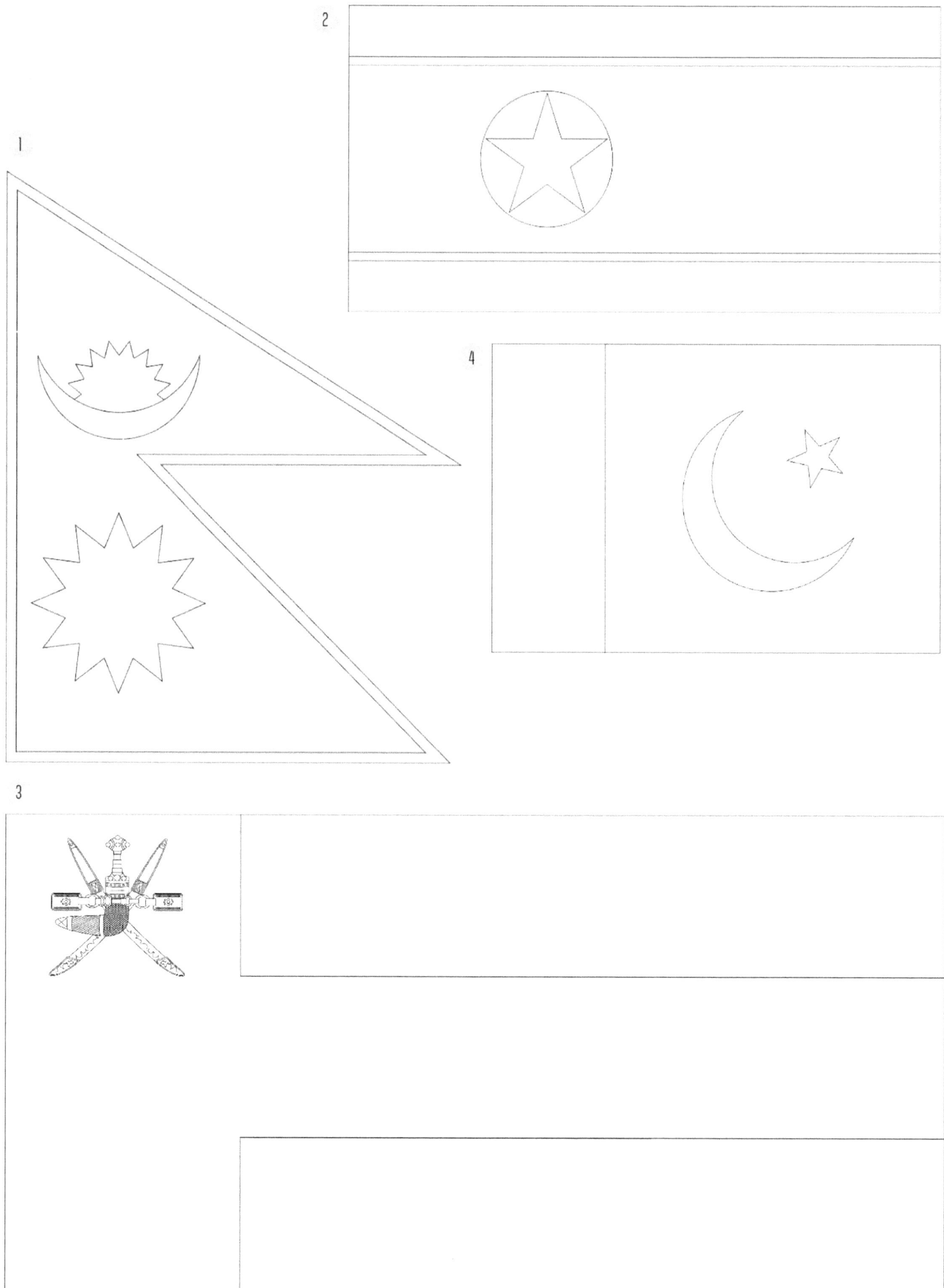

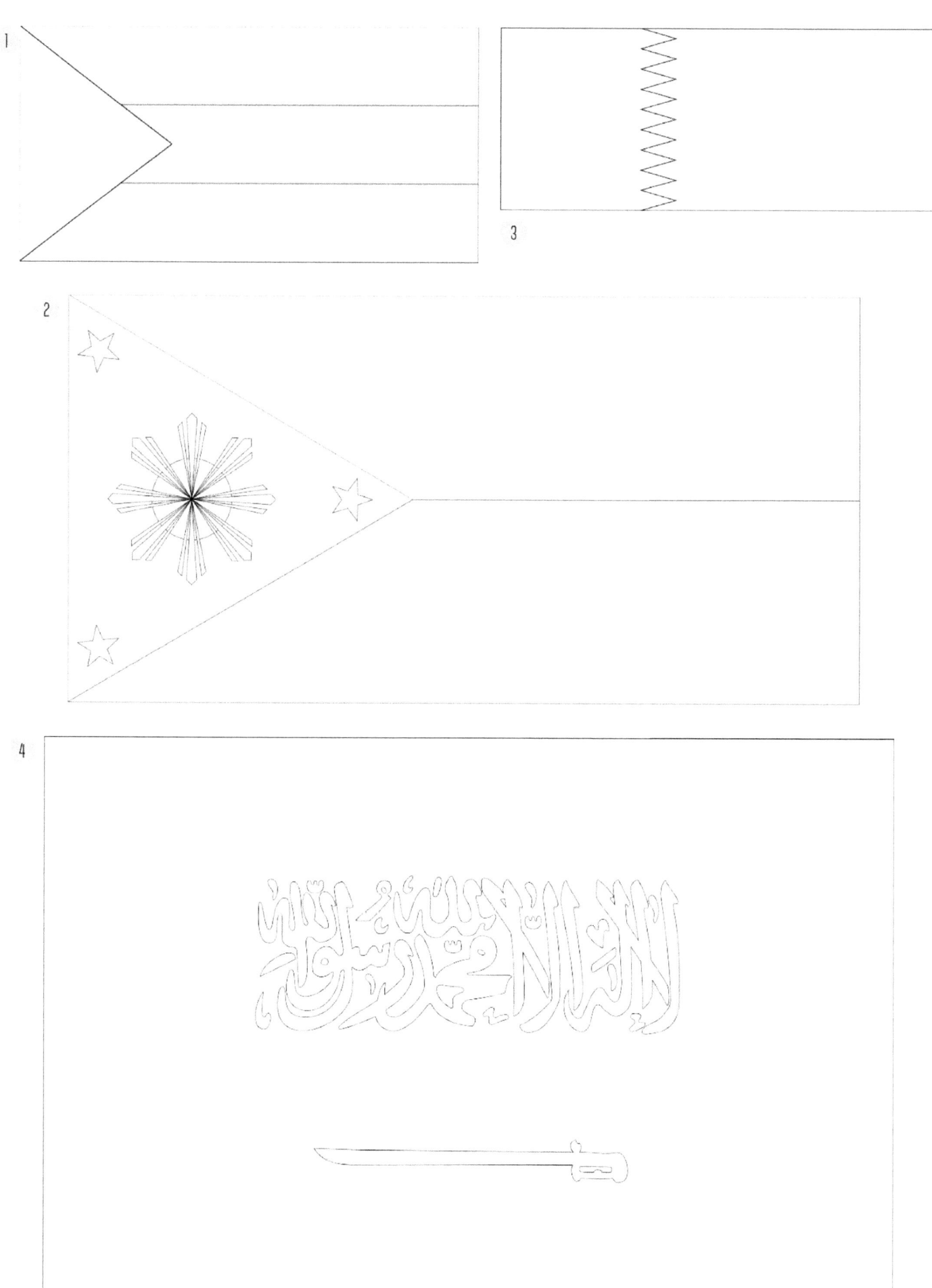

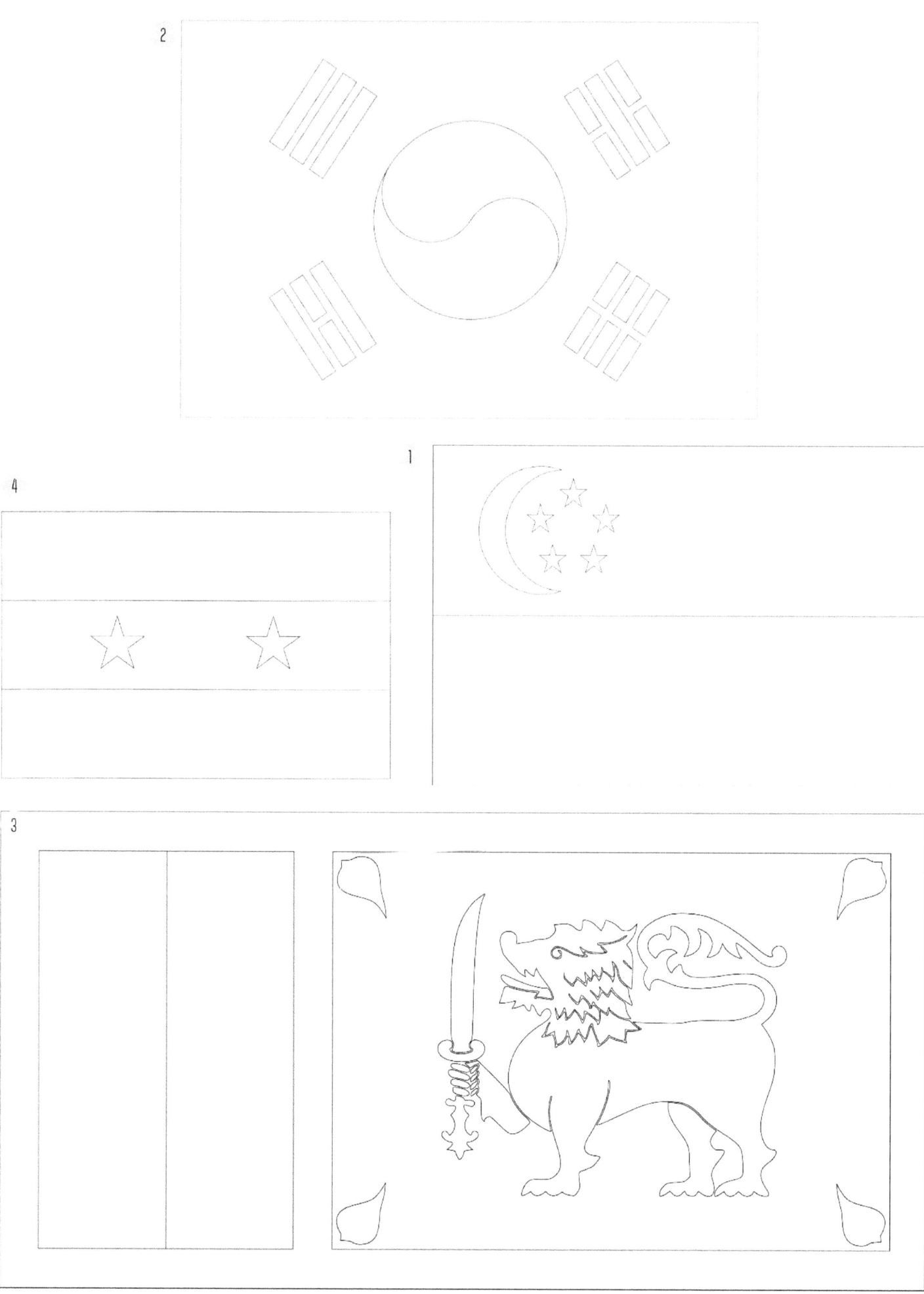

1

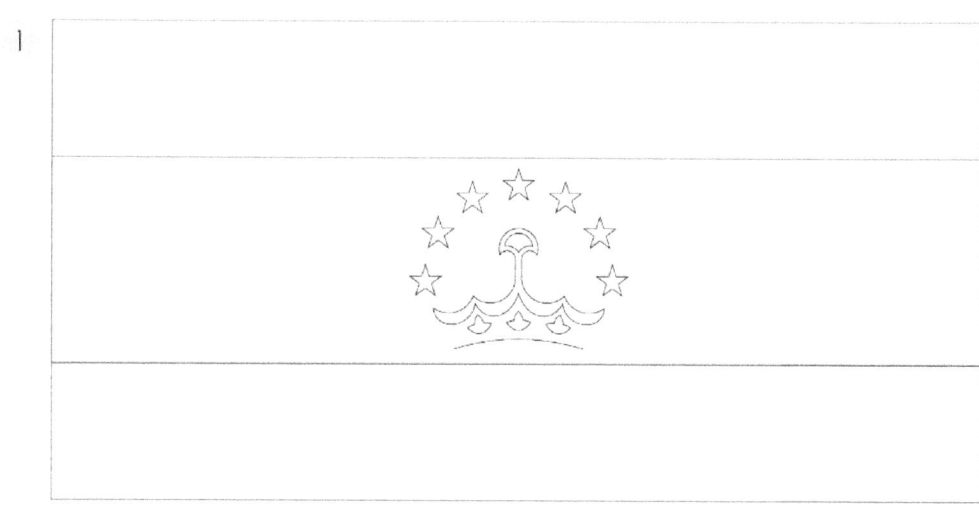

2

3

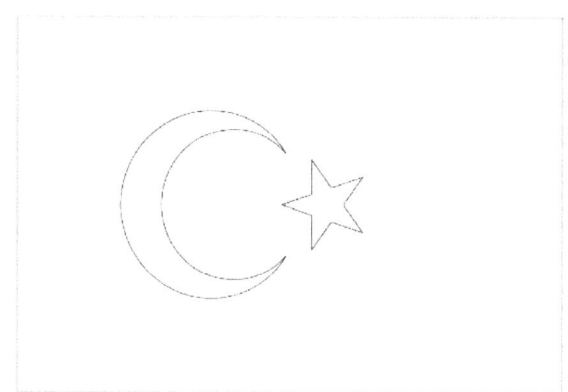

4

1 FLAG OF THE UNITED ARAB EMIRATES
3   10   15   16

2 FLAG OF UZBEKISTAN
3   8   12   16

3 FLAG OF VIETNAM
3   7

4 FLAG OF YEMEN
2   15   16

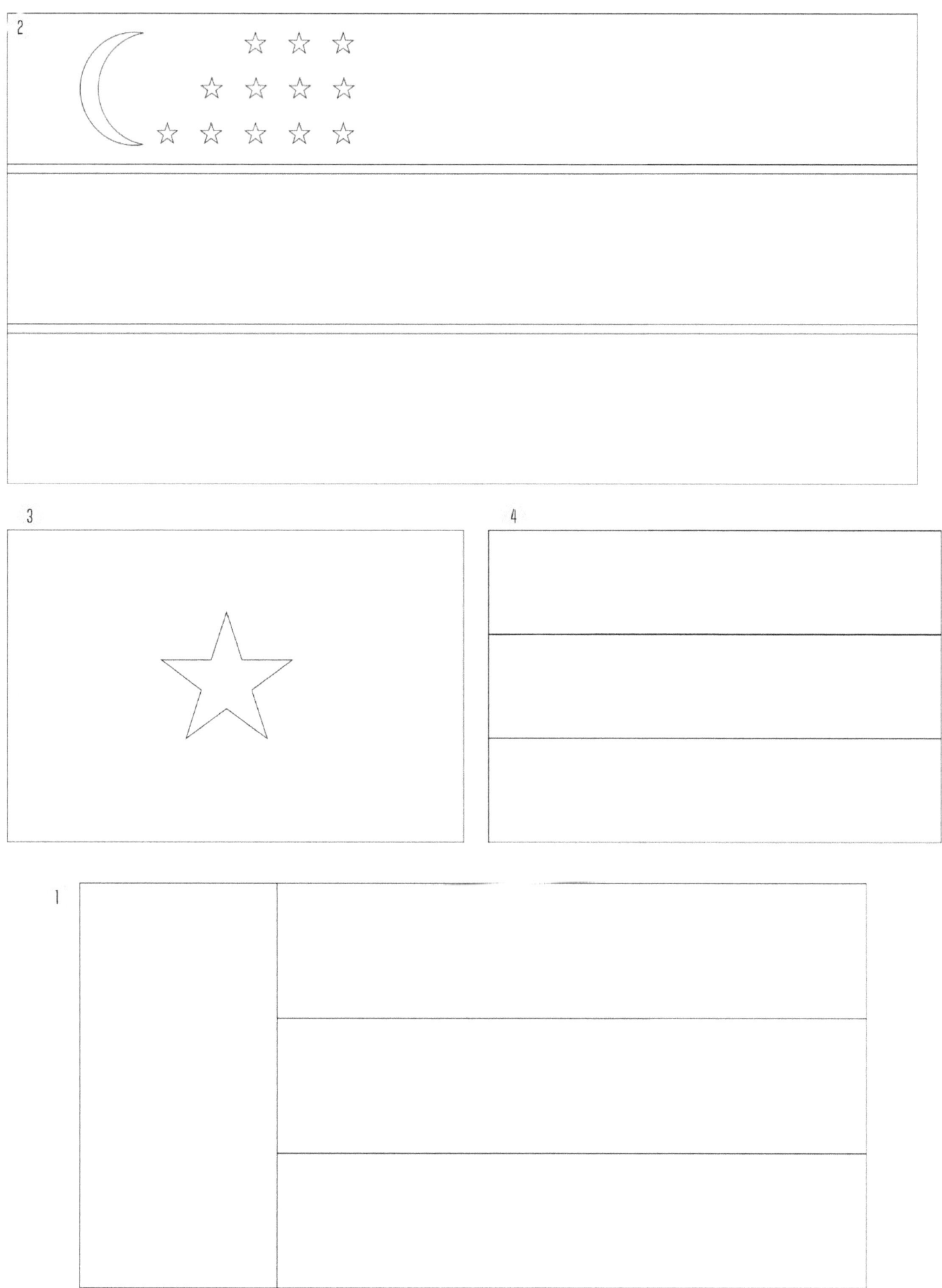

FLAGS OF OCEANIA

A-Z

1 FLAG OF AUSTRALIA
3   14   16

2 FLAG OF FIJI
3   11   14   16   *EXCLUDING COAT OF ARMS

3 FLAG OF KIRIBATI
3   11   14   16

1

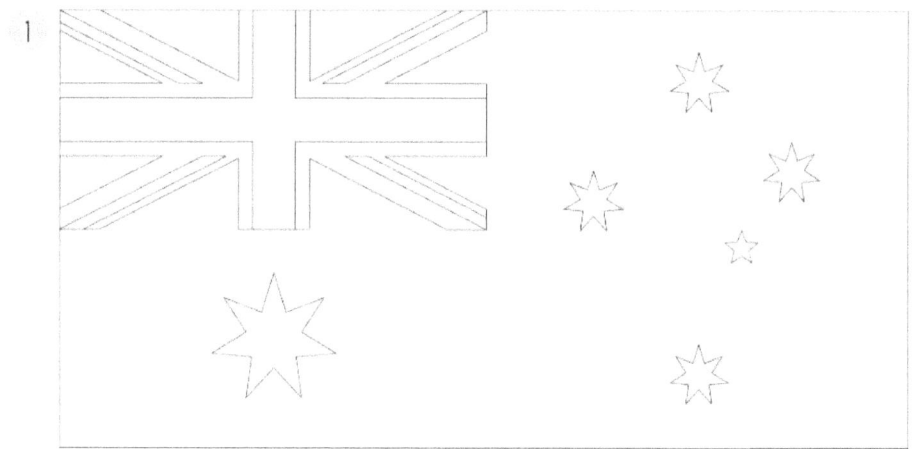

2

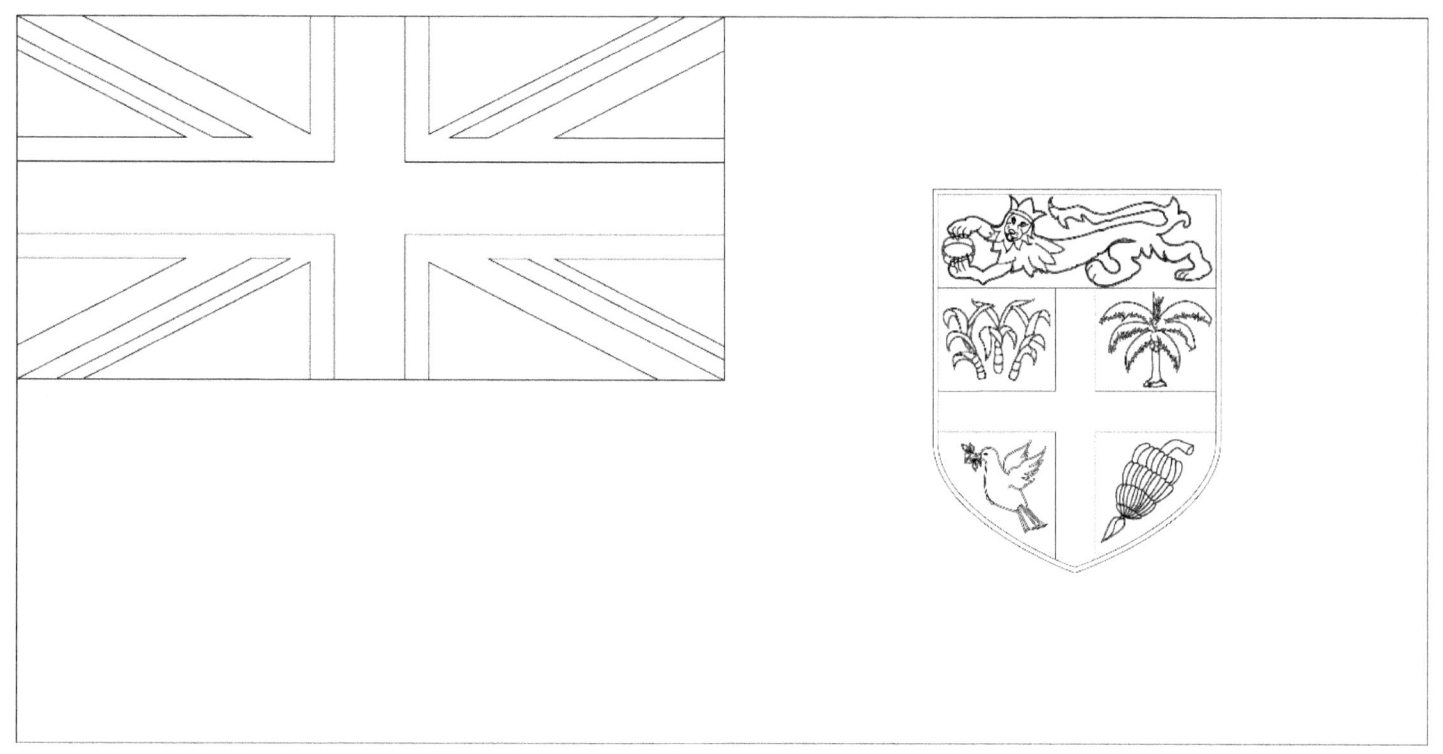

3

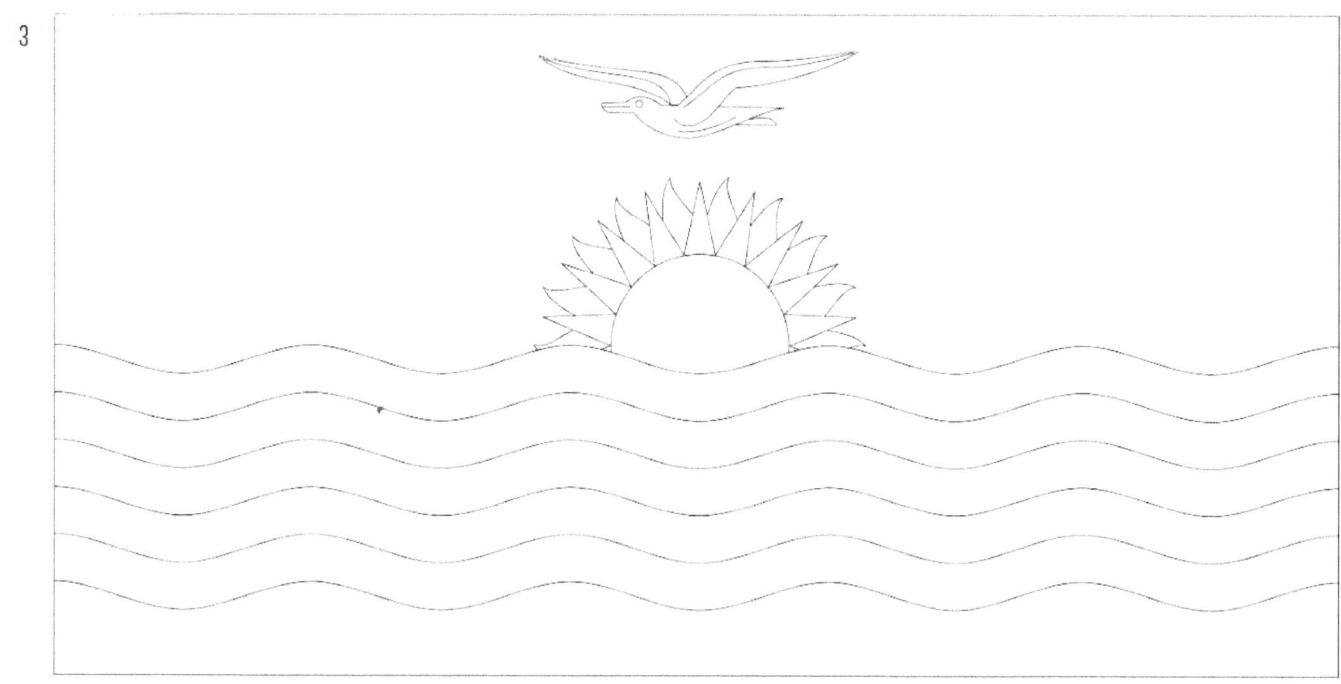

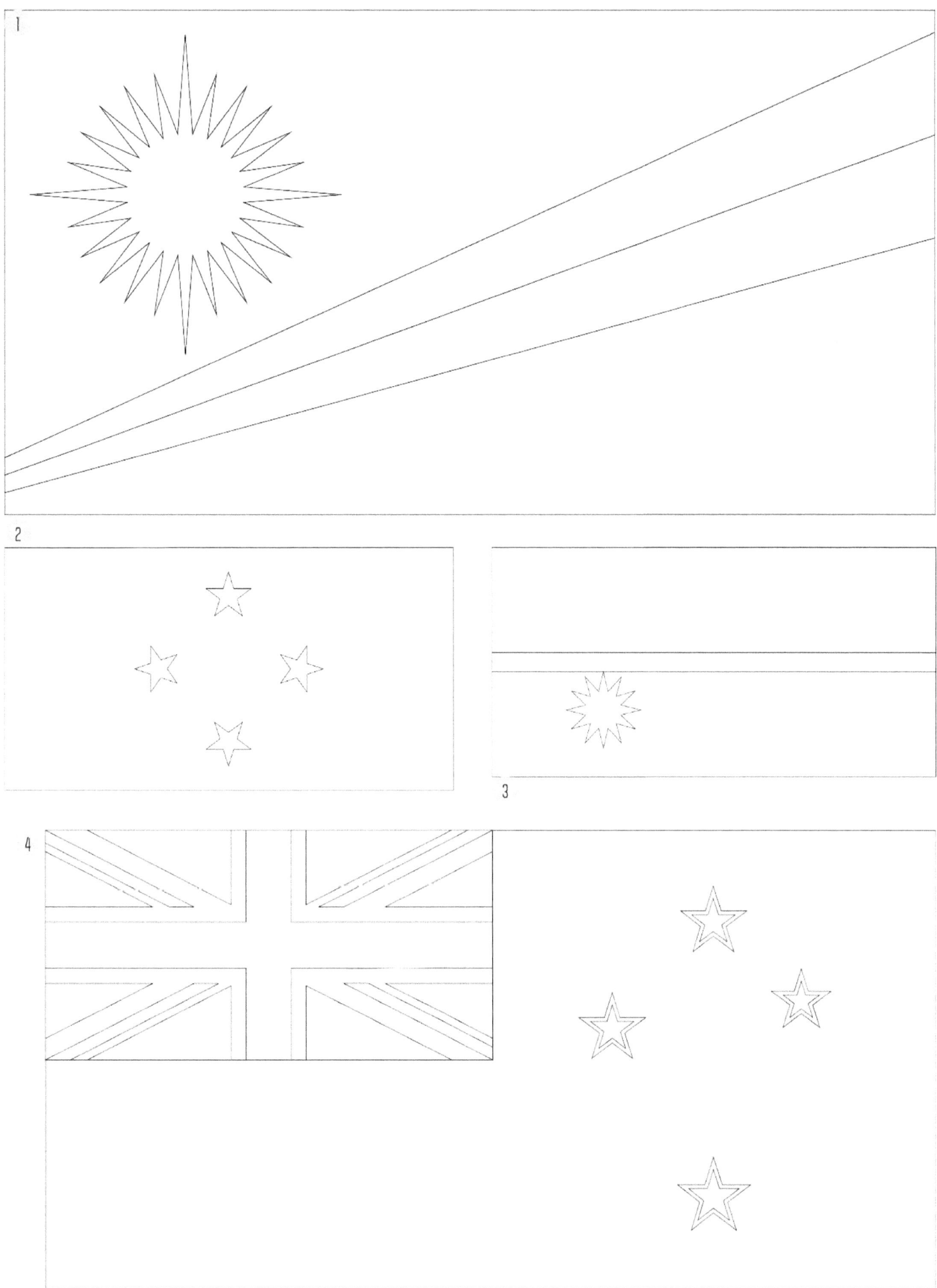

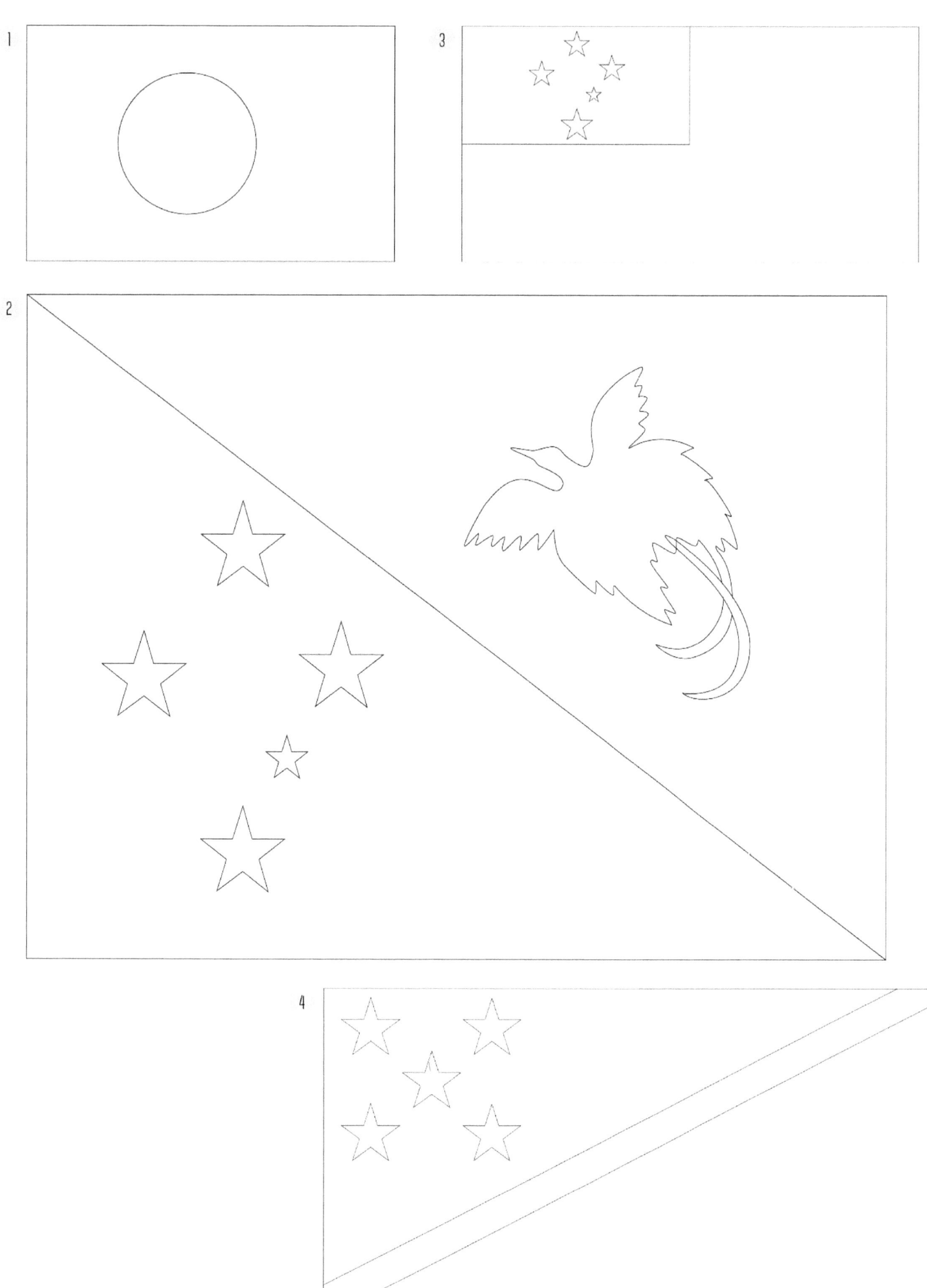

1

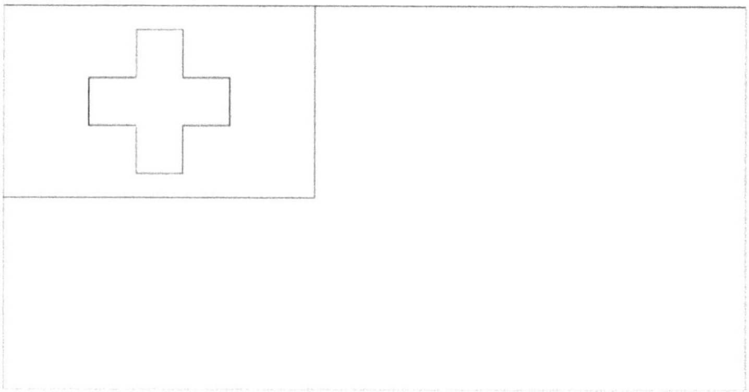

2

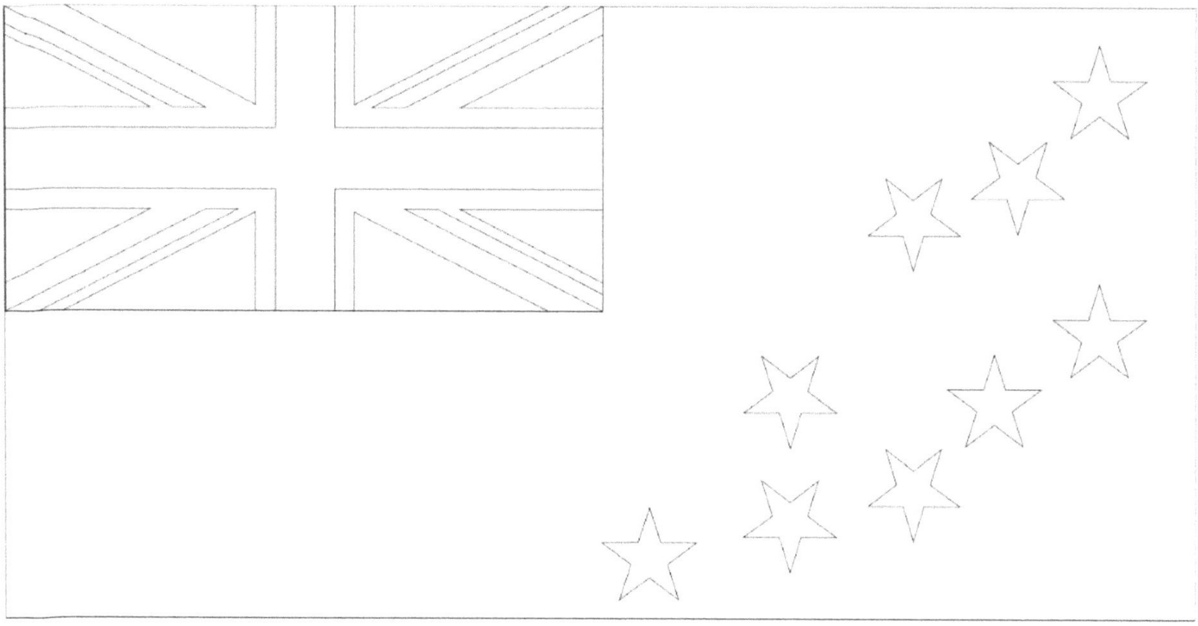

3

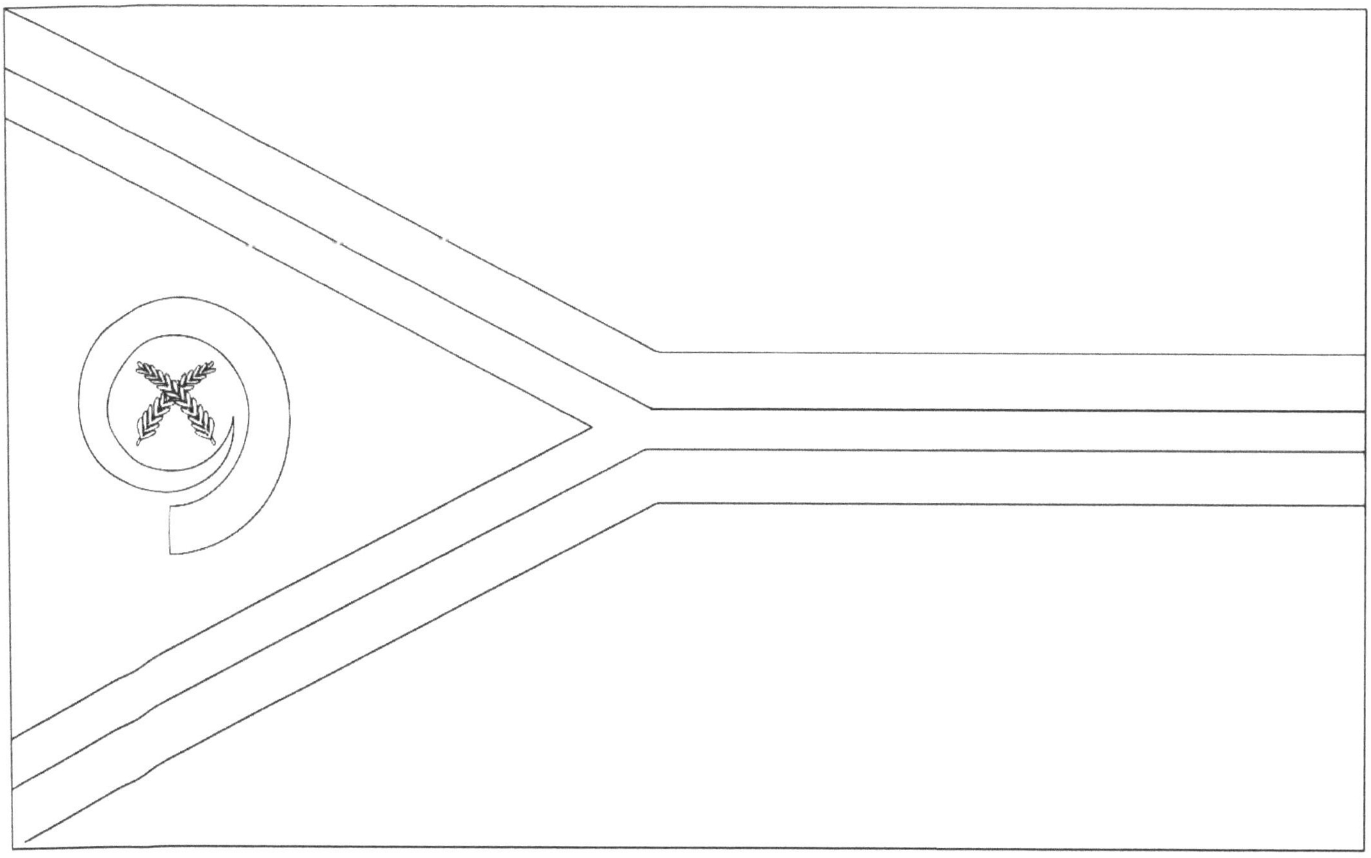

www.ingramcontent.com/pod-product-compliance
Lightning Source LLC
Chambersburg PA
CBHW081734220526
45468CB00008B/2098